# THE JOY
# OF THE LORD —
# HOW TO GET IT
# AND KEEP IT!

by
Richard Roberts

*Unless otherwise indicated,*
*all Scripture quotations are paraphrased*
*from the King James Version of the Bible.*

Copyright © 1995
by Richard Roberts
Tulsa, Oklahoma

BK 136

FIFTH PRINTING
Reprinted 10/98

# Table of Contents

# INTRODUCTION

It struck my heart like a Holy Ghost lightning bolt when a minister friend said to me, "Richard, you have a testimony that people desperately need to hear. You're already helping to revolutionize the body of Christ through this fresh baptism of joy, *but you've also learned how to* <u>*sustain*</u> *God's joy in your life!* Because of the awful gut-wrenching struggles you've been through as President of Oral Roberts University, because of the fact that ORU's debt has plunged from $42 million to $21.5 million <u>in only two years</u>, *YOUR LIFE IS LIVING PROOF THAT THE JOY OF THE LORD WORKS!"*

Then he looked at me and said, "You've got to write a book on this subject to help Christians everywhere get ahold of this explosive new revelation of the joy of the Lord! You can explain it better than anyone I know BECAUSE YOU'RE GOING THROUGH THE ROUGH WATERS ON A DAILY BASIS, <u>AND YET YOU'RE STILL FULL OF THE JOY OF THE LORD!"</u>

His words really grabbed my attention that day, and something went off in my spirit like a firecracker. Friend, this book is my personal chronicle of how the joy of the Lord came alive in my life, how Holy Ghost revival fires erupted at Oral Roberts University, *and how I became another man through this amazing new baptism of joy!*

But it's also a chronicle of ORU's exodus out of the bondage of debt. The book of Exodus in the Bible gives us a panoramic sweep of Israel's exodus from the land of Egypt. It paints a picture of the Lord's provision —

how He supplied fresh manna every day, even in the middle of the howling wilderness. **But the people had to believe for that manna to come raining down from the sky EVERY DAY.**

*I know exactly how that feels!* Over the last two years, there have been countless times when I've felt as if I were plowing a hole through the sky with my prayers, when I've stood eyeball to eyeball with the devil, trying to hold off his deathblows against ORU. *And yet at the zero hour — at the 11:59 hour — fresh manna, fresh provisions, came FLOODING down from Heaven!*

Friend, I've poured out my heart to you through this book, sharing the staggering details of how we almost lost Oral Roberts University, how God broke us free from satan's deadly grip, and how we became brand-new people in Christ THROUGH A FRESH BAPTISM OF THE JOY OF THE LORD! **I tell you, God's mighty joy and holy laughter have totally revolutionized my life!**

Do you need a brand-new, hilariously happy, Holy Ghost revolution in your life too? Do you need to learn how to laugh when there's absolutely no reason to laugh? Do you want to be filled with spontaneous, uncontrollable joy, even when the thunder is rolling and the lightning is ripping across the sky of your life? *If you do, then don't wait another moment to plunge into this book, BECAUSE I BELIEVE IT'S GOING TO REVOLUTIONIZE YOUR LIFE IN CHRIST!*

# Chapter 1

# WHEN YOU OWE $42 MILLION, THAT'S A WHOLE LOT OF ZEROES!

Oral Roberts University is the only fully accredited charismatic university in the world, with four thousand undergraduate and graduate students and over thirty thousand alumni. It was birthed as a dream in the heart of a stuttering, stammering seventeen-year-old boy named Oral Roberts as he lay dying in the backseat of a borrowed car, coughing and hemorrhaging his life away from the ravages of tuberculosis.

The papers had already been signed for him to be admitted to the sanitarium in Talihina, Oklahoma. But that night he was on his way to a great healing service in Pontotoc County, Oklahoma, where a man of God was praying for the sick, *and people were being loosed from the grip of death itself!*

As he rode along in that car, my father could hear the voices of my Uncle Elmer and my grandmother, Claudius Priscilla Roberts, talking through the darkness. They were telling stories of an old-time gospel meeting, *a meeting where even a person with the terrible dreaded disease of tuberculosis had been healed that very week!*

My dad heard another voice whispering in his ear that night, the voice of almighty God, saying to him,

"Son, I am going to heal you, and you are to take My healing power to your generation. *And someday you are to build Me a university.*"

At the close of that gospel meeting, my father's stuttering tongue was healed and the tuberculosis was driven from his body through the prayers of an evangelist who believed God could do anything. Raised up from a literal deathbed, my father was called to preach. A spark was ignited in his heart to build God a university based upon His authority and the power of the Holy Spirit. All through the years of the great tent healing campaigns my father conducted, he held on to that dream.

As the years flew by, something like a magnet kept drawing my dad to a choice piece of ground in south Tulsa, Oklahoma. My mind flashes back to all the times when I was a boy and we would drive along Lewis Avenue until we came to a stop in front of that piece of property. My father believed that God had preserved that land for a holy cause — so that a great university might be raised up to the glory of God.

Many years after God spoke to a boy named Oral Roberts in the backseat of a borrowed car, there was another boy whose story is inextricably woven into the fabric of Oral Roberts University — a boy who roamed this piece of ground where ORU now stands, carrying a fishing pole and a baseball bat, a boy without a care in the world. If you let him play all day long, he was happy. He was in his own little world. Really, he was a lot like young David in the Bible . . . *a boy whom nobody thought would amount to anything!*

I'm sure you recall the remarkable story of David. God had commanded the prophet Samuel to anoint a new king over the nation of Israel. So Samuel journeyed to Bethlehem, to the house of Jesse, searching for a successor to the throne. As each one of Jesse's sons — David's brothers — passed by Samuel, he exclaimed, "No, he's not the one!" *You see, David had completely slipped everybody's mind!* But he was the one God had chosen to be king! (See I Samuel 16.)

Friend, that's the story of my life too! I was the "David" in my family. I was that little boy with a bat and a ball and a fishing pole, trudging home from school with my shirttail torn and dirty, swinging my lunch pail, and whistling a song I'd made up. Everybody thought it would be my older brother who would preach the Gospel. *No one seemed to give me a second thought!* But you can't figure out God! *HE HAD A DIFFERENT PLAN FOR MY LIFE!*

## THE LORD SAID TO MY FATHER, "BUILD ME A UNIVERSITY!"

As a young man, I was walking down the wrong road, rebellious to my parents and irreverent to the Lord. There was a huge wall that loomed between my dad and me. But I'll never forget as long as I live the summer he wrote to me while I was at Interlochen National Music Camp in Traverse City, Michigan, and told me that God had spoken to him again about the newly opened Oral Roberts University.

The Lord's words to my father were: "Raise up your students to hear My voice, to go where My light is dim, where My voice is heard small, and My healing power is not known . . . even to the uttermost bounds of the earth. Their work will exceed yours, and in this I am well pleased."

9

It was a dangerous time in the United States of America when Oral Roberts launched out to build a university to the glory of God. It was in the middle of the violent sixties, when the civil rights movement was in full swing and racial tensions had reached a fever pitch. It was at the height of the hippie movement, when young people were defying all authority, disrupting society in a violent way.

It was a restless antiestablishment era in this country, with the protests raging against the Vietnam War. Crowds were marching in the streets. American flags were being flung to the ground and burned. The National Guard was gunning down student protesters on university campuses. It was an unpredictable time to build a university with a Prayer Tower as its centerpiece and to boldly proclaim that above all the books of academic learning, **the number one book is the Holy Bible.**

It was a dangerous time in my life too. You see, even though I was raised on the Bible, I was not a Christian. I, too, was caught up in the growing tide of rebellion that was sweeping America's youth. I was a runaway from God and also from my parents.

I thought I was having the time of my life as a young person, getting involved in just about everything a teenager can get involved in. In the spring of 1967, I came home from the university I was attending for ORU's dedication. I'll never forget how jolted I was by the words Billy Graham spoke that day, just a few months before my nineteenth birthday. He declared, "If this institution ever moves away from faith in the Bible, and faith in God, and putting God first, *then let us this day pronounce a curse on it!*" **I've never been able to get away from those**

**words!**

Later, his words kept ringing in my heart until I finally obeyed the voice of the Lord when He told me that I was supposed to be a student at ORU. After I transferred here, I can remember watching in amazement as some of my dad's Partners pulled into the parking lot in front of Claudius Roberts Dormitory, climbed out of their car on a scorching-hot, 100-degree day and, with tears rolling down their cheeks, stooped down and kissed the pavement!

Then I heard one of them exclaim breathlessly, "Oh, I can feel Jesus on these grounds!" I tell you, that experience is forever branded in my spirit! And it wasn't long — only a matter of a few weeks — before I gave my heart to the Lord!

## ORAL ROBERTS UNIVERSITY IS HAZARDOUS TO THE DEVIL'S HEALTH!

All throughout the years, it seems as if the devil has singled out Oral Roberts University, blasting us with his entire arsenal from hell. Now if I were the devil, I would single out ORU too! Why? Because this place is dangerous to satan. It's hazardous to his health! But even more than that, ORU is precious. It's precious to God and also to the body of Christ. After all, where else on the face of this earth are you going to find a fully accredited, academically outstanding, charismatic, Bible-believing university with both undergraduate and graduate schools, where young people can "get their learnin' and keep their burnin'" *and also learn how to hear God's voice?*

Yes, there are many other first-rate, Bible-believing

Christian colleges throughout this nation and around the world, *and I praise God for them!* **But ORU is special.** **EVEN OUR DETRACTORS ADMIT THERE'S NO OTHER PLACE IN THE WORLD LIKE THIS PLACE! Academics, Holy Ghost prayer, and healthy physical education and aerobics, all in one university!**

Really, it was no great surprise to me when satan launched an all-out assault against ORU in the summer of 1993. *And I believe the devil thought he had us by the throat!* Why? Because of a $42-million debt which was wrapped around our necks like a gigantic ball and chain!

Now before 1987, there was <u>no</u> significant debt against ORU or our ministry. But during that year, several scandals struck the body of Christ which involved well-known television ministries. These incidents were magnified by the news media to such outrageous proportions that virtually every ministry, every church, every Christian school, was hit — *and we were hit hard!* Almost overnight a skepticism sprang up in the hearts of people all across America concerning giving to God's work.

As a result, many Christian schools and churches were struggling. Many ministries simply could not withstand the brutal financial pressure. Even those of us who had nothing to do with the various scandals were shaken by terrible losses. And Oral Roberts University took a blow so crushing that it's an absolute miracle we remained standing.

*When those scandals rocked the church world in 1987, our income was slashed by 50 percent <u>in only thirty days</u>!* For the first time ever, ORU and our ministry began a slide into debt. Between 1987 and

1993, we tightened our belt, cut a number of programs, and significantly reduced the size of our staff. We were working our hearts out to be the very best stewards of God's money that we could be, *and yet we were still floundering, and the debt was growing.*

By the time my father, Oral Roberts, officially stepped down as President and Chief Executive Officer of Oral Roberts University in January 1993, our debt had skyrocketed to $42 million! Now $42 million IS a large amount of money, but it's not such a staggering figure when you consider our debt-to-asset ratio. Many universities would be thrilled to have ORU's debt-to-asset ratio. However, it was still a debt of $42 million, and we had no earthly way to pay it!

It was my father's highest dream that all the indebtedness against ORU would be wiped out by the end of his thirty years of tenure. He had told me, "Richard, I want you to start with a clean slate!" It was certainly a worthy dream, *but somehow it was just beyond our fingertips!*

When my father announced to the Board of Regents that he would not stand for reelection, he told them, "I recommend my son, Richard, to be your new President, *but it's your decision."* Now no one knew who the board's choice would be because they are an autonomous group. They were free to elect whomever they chose. However, when the appointed time came, the Chairman of the Board, Marilyn Hickey, a dear woman of God, opened the floor for nominations, and my name was placed into nomination. Then the nominations were closed.

It was my desire to "shoot straight" with the board right from the start, so I asked the chairman if I could say a word before they voted. "If you're casting your vote for me because I'm Oral Roberts' son, I do not wish to be President of this university," I said. *"However, if you believe I'm God's man for the job, then I want to be your next President."*

The vote was cast, and it was unanimous in my favor. So we marched across the campus to Christ's Chapel for an installation service before the entire faculty, staff, and student body. I accepted my new position with fear and trepidation — not in the sense of being terrified by it, *but in holy fear and reverence for the Lord.*

The newspapers flashed the headlines the next day: "The Torch Is Passed!" And after they hung a big medallion around my neck, *they handed me the $42-million debt.* Friend, do you know what it feels like to owe $42 million? I certainly hope not! But it's not much different from owing $40,000 or $4,000 — if you don't have the money to pay it! You can put the decimal point anywhere you want to put it, **but debt is still debt!**

My father had already told me, "Richard, when I step down as president, your mother and I are going to stay out of the picture as much as possible. I've been ORU's leader for so long that people will try to get around you to get to me. Out of respect for you as the new leader, your mother and I will no longer be active in the university's operations. But I will be available if you need me."

The first few months were a time of getting my feet wet. It was a time to learn. For although I thought I was prepared, nothing quite prepares you to be the president of a university.

As the first few months passed, the Lord led me to

make some leadership changes. These were not bad people; they were just out of step with the mission of ORU, and they had to go. By June the pressure began to mount. Creditors were coming out of the wood-work. Our bankers were all over me. We couldn't make our payments and pay our bills. Too much month at the end of the money. I started sinking lower and lower. Have you ever gotten really low? I mean, you talk about having the the bottom fall out — the stress of a $9-million-a-year debt service alone was eating up my insides!

<u>Meanwhile, I felt like the whole world was watching</u>! It seemed as if people all across America were speculating about what Richard Roberts would do next — *whether or not I would depart from ORU's founding purpose.*

The naysayers had prophesied for many years that no one would be able to maintain Oral Roberts University when my father was no longer active in its admin-istration. They insisted that ORU would fall by the wayside, that it would become a secular university.

The devil tried to show me a day when there would be no Prayer Tower at Oral Roberts University, a day when there would be no Holy Spirit-filled chapel services, no uncompromising stand upon the Word of God, no power of prayer. He tried to show me a day when the faculty would be allowed to run wild and publish anything they wanted to, whether or not it was in harmony with the power of the Holy Spirit and the founding purpose of the university. *And that thought sent shivers up and down my backbone!*

Yes, satan was bombarding me with images of ORU going the way of many other universities in this country which originally were founded upon the power of God, *but now they're mere shadows of their beginnings.* The devil sneered at me, "It took your father thirty years to build this university, <u>*but I'm going to destroy it in one year through you!*</u>" I awakened in the night from dreams of newspaper headlines saying everything was going under. And, in the natural, it looked like satan was right on target!

I mean, we were going from pillar to post in our finances. I was making regular trips downtown to see our bankers, and every time I came out of their offices, I felt as if I had blood running down my face *because of the ghastly financial beating I was taking.* Really, I felt like I was a fireman. **I was spending my entire life putting out fires!**

By July it seemed as if my whole life was disintegrating! The weight of the problem was so colossal, so overwhelming, that I decided God couldn't possibly carry it by Himself, SO I TRIED TO HELP HIM! Now I understood that He was God, but sometimes we humans try to shoulder our own load, even though we know that Jesus said, *"Cast your burden upon Me. I can carry it!"* (see I Peter 5:7).

In the meantime, my wife was seeing the change in me. She said that I was angry all the time! My stomach was tied up in knots. I had developed an ulcer. Everything inside me was always churning, and no matter what I did, I couldn't seem to settle down. Resting and sleeping became increasingly difficult.

I had become an unholy terror! My attitude had gone right down the tubes. The initial happiness and elation I had felt when I was elected President of ORU had turned into a dark scowl. I wanted to run away.

And yet I wanted God so much! I was pacing the floor, back and forth, crying out in the night, my body shaking in agony. I was calling on the Lord, stretching myself out to Him, desperately grappling with my faith. There were times when I had to literally put my Bible on the floor and stand on it. *By faith,* I was standing on the Word of God, believing that He would shatter the devil's blow against Oral Roberts University!

As I cried out to the Lord, suddenly He began to draw my attention to several areas of the university where we had somehow gotten off track. Immediately, I began to deal with those situations, and eventually I had to assume the responsibilities of chief financial officer <u>in order to deal with our creditors personally</u>.

Then I began to meet personally with representatives from those companies, and I laid my cards on the table. I refused to make any false promises. Instead, I asked them for favor. I asked them to help us devise a plan for repaying those debts. They knew I needed time, and most of them confided to me, "Richard, we just wanted somebody who would return our phone calls!" <u>Then we began to search for ways to pay them off a little bit at a time!</u>

Friend, it was so humiliating not to be able to pay all of our bills! We had always maintained an outstanding record with our creditors, *and now it seemed as if the bills were piling higher and higher, yet the money to pay them was barely trickling in! The Partners who had stayed with us when the crisis hit were extremely faithful in their giving. It just wasn't enough to pay the bills and service the debt!*

17

## GOD WILL NOT
## OVERLOOK OUR SEED!

I made another discovery that summer which hit me like a freight train! Somehow, in the middle of all the rough financial waters, the decision had been made to cut off our corporate giving. Now Lindsay and I had never stopped our personal tithing, but our financial staff had become so concerned with hoarding every penny that they had completely shut down our ministry's giving to other ministries and works of the Lord!

I can't describe how horrified I was when I made that shocking discovery! <u>You see</u>, <u>when you stop tithing, the windows of Heaven are suddenly slammed shut</u>. Without any warning, you're left standing out in the cold, wondering why your windows of blessing are closed up tight. In the meantime, the devourer (the devil) is not rebuked, *and he's running roughshod over your entire life!* (See Malachi 3:10,11.)

The instant I uncovered this shattering piece of information, I led ORU and our ministry in a corporate time of repentance before the Lord. Then I gathered my administrative team together and told them, "I don't care how much it hurts or how impossible it looks in the natural, *we're going to give 10 percent of our daily income as tithes unto the Lord.*"

They agreed with me 100 percent even though they knew how difficult it would be. **<u>By the Spirit, we all knew that tithing was our only hope of crawling out from under that avalanche of bills</u>**!

By ten o'clock every morning we had received word about our income for that day, and <u>each day</u> we started faithfully sowing 10 percent of our income to God. *All across this nation and around the world, we began to SOW, SOW, SOW!*

I remember one particular week when we sent a Seed-Faith offering to a ministry in New Mexico, and the woman who is the head of that organization telephoned my office and burst into tears as she asked my secretary, "How did Richard know that today was the day they were going to turn off our lights?"

When my secretary related her message to me, I replied quickly, "Tell her that Richard didn't know, **but God knew!**"

> *I tell you, the instant we started tithing again, it seemed as if a dam broke loose in the spirit realm, and suddenly the miracles started raining down!*

Not long after we had reinstituted our tithing, I was preaching in a great church in California, baring my heart to them concerning the gut-wrenching trials I had been going through. At the close of the service, the Spirit of God began moving through the pastor, and he gave me a very reassuring word from the Lord. He said that because of my faithfulness in tithing, I was going to be greeted with some thrilling news when I returned home!

Well, it was only a day or two later when I received word from an attorney on the East Coast about a very large donation which had been left to the university by one of our long-standing Partners. Of course, the will would have to go through probate court, which would take time, *but I knew that sum of money was coming at that time as a direct result of our tithes and offerings to the Lord!*

For one fleeting moment, I caught a glimpse of God up in Heaven flinging open the windows of blessings of the invisible realm! *And all of a sudden, I had an overwhelming desire to sow my seeds to Him ten feet deep! Why? BECAUSE GOD HAS DECLARED THROUGH HIS SON, JESUS CHRIST, <u>THAT HE WILL NOT OVER-LOOK OUR SEED!</u>*

## Chapter 2

# THE SUMMER ORAL ROBERTS UNIVERSITY ALMOST WENT DOWN THE TUBES

It was "hell on wheels" that first brutal summer as President of ORU. I can recall several specific times when there was absolutely no way for us to meet the payroll. And yet every time the devil slammed our backs against the wall, _we continued planting our seeds as though it was going out of style, **and God turned satan away from the door**_!

It's forever branded in my mind the time we had to have $1.1 million within only a few days or we could kiss the whole thing good-bye! You see, a certain group was planning to file a lien against ORU, but I had convinced them to give me a thirty-day "stay of execution" so I could try to raise the money.

Friend, can you imagine what the headlines splattered across the newspapers would look like if somebody slapped a $1.1 million lien on ORU? Can you imagine how that story could get twisted by the TV news? Oh, the sensationalism!

As we gathered around the conference table for our management meeting that Tuesday, our faces were deathly solemn. Actually, we were almost in a state of shock! We knew what was looming before us, but we had no idea where the answer was coming from. A strong word of prophecy came forth that day, commanding us to stand still and see the salvation of the Lord.

But when the deadline hit a few days later, <u>we still didn't have the $1.1 million</u>! I had raised a significant portion of it, *but not the full amount.* So I arranged for a meeting with a representative of that group, desperately hoping they would accept the money I had raised in lieu of the full amount. But the man replied, "Cannot do!"

As he was on his way out the door to go to the courthouse to file the lien, he turned to me and said, "If you can get the rest of the money by 8:30 tomorrow morning, **<u>the lien can be removed before anyone sees it</u>.**"

I was exceedingly grateful for that piece of information, and when I got back to my office, I had an old-time, Holy Ghost prayer meeting with the Lord! I mean, I was praying fervently, earnestly, with tears bursting from my eyes, *BECAUSE IT LOOKED AS THOUGH IT WAS ALL OVER FOR ORAL ROBERTS UNIVERSITY!*

Lo and behold, just a few minutes later, my secretary buzzed me and said that one of our ORU graduates from Oklahoma City was outside waiting to see me. It was a young man whom I had helped get through ORU on a music scholarship, and he had gone on to become a music minister for a church in Oklahoma City. Now I didn't have a clue as to what he wanted, but I was still happy to see him. So I told my secretary, "Sure, send him in!"

When that young man walked into my office, he had a peculiar look on his face. "Richard," he said slowly, "I did some work for a man in Oklahoma City, and he asked me to deliver this gift to you for the university." And then he handed me an envelope. When I opened that envelope, my eyes came out on stems! *Inside was a check for $1 million for Oral Roberts University!*

I laughed, I cried, I jumped, I screamed, and I hollered. I grabbed that guy, and we did a hallelujah dance all around my office, waving that $1-million check in the air! And then I rushed right down to deliver the money to our creditor, <u>and at eight-thirty the next morning, they removed the lien which had been filed against ORU at five o'clock the previous day</u>!

---

**Friend, I don't believe it's any coincidence that this miracle occurred within thirty days after we had reinstituted our tithing!**

---

My mind goes back to another crisis which erupted during that first horrible summer as President of ORU. You see, a certain bank debt was unexpectedly called in for payment, and we were scrambling to pay it, *but there was just no way!* So I rushed downtown to meet with the leadership of that bank, and I poured out my heart to them concerning the harrowing details of what I'd been through that summer.

Much to my astonishment, they told me, "Richard, there was a time when Oral Roberts University stood with our bank when <u>we</u> had a need. *Now we're going to stand with you.*" And that bank actually loaned us the money to pay off that debt! I tell you, that's the amazing grace of Jesus Christ *in action!* In the ensuing months, God blessed us doubly, *and we were able to wipe out that entire debt!*

Every time another bill was staring us in the face, satan would rear his ugly head and sneer, "You've made it so far, **but you will not make it this time."** Then we'd slip all the way out to the edge — you know what I mean by "the edge" — with absolutely no prospect of deliverance. And somehow, out of the blue, God would bail us out!

I have never prayed, "Give us this day our daily bread," in such deadly earnest as I did that first summer as President of ORU. It was like gathering manna from Heaven — *ONE DAY AT A TIME! THERE WERE SIMPLY NO LEFTOVERS!*

## I COULD READ THE HANDWRITING ON THE WALL!

In spite of all the unbelievable miracles God performed for us, **by the time fall rolled around, it looked as though we would have to close the doors of ORU.** I had been fighting my heart out, spiritually wrestling demonic powers all summer long. But no matter how feverishly we worked and sweated and prayed, IT STILL LOOKED AS THOUGH ORU WAS GOING DOWN FOR THE COUNT!

Now there was another issue which I was also facing at that time. You see, all of my life I've felt as if I were living in a glass house. Even as a young boy, I was under the most intense scrutiny. I was constantly being badgered with comments such as, "Oh, you're Oral Roberts' son! How are you ever going to fill his shoes?"

And I can remember so vividly when I was a boy how I would stuff tissues into the toes of my dad's shoes so I could keep them from flopping off my feet when I tried them on. *BUT HIS SHOES WERE TOO BIG FOR ME!* You know, when you're the son of a man who has accomplished something extraordinary in his life, you face a hard road. Everybody wonders about you. *Everybody speculates about whether or not you'll ever be able to fill your father's shoes!*

But a long time ago, I came to grips with the fact that my size 9-1/2 foot is never going to fill my dad's size 11 shoes! *But I can fill my own shoes all the way to the toes!* And God doesn't expect us to fill anybody else's shoes! **He expects us to be what He created us to be!**

The harder I fought to drive the wolves away from ORU's doors, the more I felt as if my knees were buckling under the load! My mind was screaming, "What if I fail?" And I believe the fear of failure is perhaps even more paralyzing than failure itself. Why? Because the fear of failure is like falling asleep with the TV on. When you wake up, it's still droning in the background. The fear of failure is constantly swirling around in your head, *mocking and taunting you day and night!*

*Friend, I could read the handwriting on the wall!* I knew that satan had ORU in a deadly stranglehold. And he was <u>determined</u> to snuff out the dream my father had sweated his life's blood to build!

Oh, how I wished they had never elected me president in the first place! If only my father had remained president for a few more years! Then, if satan had carried out his death threat against ORU, he could have done it under my dad's tenure and not mine!

I was positively miserable. I was like a rubber band that was stretched taut all the time. Day after day, I was haunted by images of padlocks swinging from the university's doors. I could even picture the sheriff's auction, with the bankers coming in to take over and the creditors swarming like vultures all over our property. In my mind's eye, I could see us conducting the biggest garage sale the world has ever known!

*The devil had painted a grim picture for me. I just knew I was going to get blamed for my daddy's dream going down the tubes!*

## RICHARD HAD BECOME A TERRIBLE PAIN IN THE NECK!

I'm proud to have a wife who stands beside me as a true Bible wife in every sense of the word — as my helpmate, the mother of my children, my sweetheart, and my partner in the healing Gospel of Jesus. Lindsay has stood by my side faithfully through the good times as well as the bad. *And she's been with me every step of the way through this terrible ordeal!*

Now I know she is too dignified to tell you some of the stories she could tell, but I've asked her to share in her own words just how miserable I had become before the joy of the Lord came into my life:

*After thirteen years of marriage to Richard — thirteen of the most glorious years of my life — all at once the pressure of being President of ORU started shoving him down until it seemed like he was living at* *the bottom of the barrel. When I looked at my precious husband, all I could see was a $42-million debt wrapped around his neck like a ball and chain!*

*I watched this man, who has never been the type to get overwhelmed by anything, as he began to sink lower and lower. He was caught in the grip of a yoke of bondage — BOUND BY THE DEBT AT ORAL ROBERTS UNIVERSITY!*

*Every day I saw Richard slipping deeper into a pit of depression. I saw nights when he never slept, days when he never ate. I saw all the times that he <u>didn't</u> spend with his children, **and he had always been very attentive to his children.** <u>Really, it seemed as if my Richard was gone and a total stranger had come into our household in my husband's body</u>.*

*The debt, the pressure, the obstacles, had begun to consume his entire life. It was sheer torture watching him suffer and feeling so helpless as he sank lower and lower into the pit.*

*My practical jokes have always been funny to Richard, but suddenly even I couldn't make him laugh! **Nothing was funny to him anymore!** The huge mountain of problems began to overwhelm him, pushing him down, down, down. My Richard was gone, and I didn't know how on earth to get him back!*

*You see, my husband had a heavy heart. Proverbs 17:22 says, "A broken spirit drieth the bones." I believe Richard's bones were drying up from the inside out. And he definitely had a broken spirit. **<u>It seemed as if everything about him was broken!</u>***

*Every morning he went through terrible financial struggles at ORU, and then the rest of the day I would see him walking around like a zombie! Just about the time he thought he had heard the worst possible news, someone would zap him with another piece of news that was even more horrifying! It seemed like the troubles at ORU were driving him into the ground!*

*Then one day the devil started talking to my husband, saying, "In less than one year I'm going to destroy what it took your father thirty years to build!" And do you know what? At that point, <u>in the natural</u>, <u>it appeared that's exactly what was going to happen!</u>*

*No matter how hard we tried to believe God, we couldn't seem to make even a tiny dent in that gigantic wall of debt. We couldn't chip away at it. We couldn't see the end of it. We couldn't see a way around it. We couldn't penetrate it. It was like banging our heads against a solid brick wall. We were getting absolutely nowhere!*

*Then one day it hit me:* **Richard is slipping away from us. He's so overwhelmed by this debt that he doesn't notice anything or anyone else.** *I mean, he couldn't see me. He couldn't see the kids. That $42-million debt was the only thing looming before him.*

*For instance, I'll never forget the night I almost blew myself up. You see, we have a gas grill in our house, and I had turned on the pilot light so I could light the grill, but I didn't realize I had turned the gas up too high. When I lit the torch, I literally blew myself all the way across the room and slammed into the wall!*

*Thank God, I wasn't killed, but when I reached up and ran my fingers through my hair, a huge hunk of hair came off in my hand! I had blown the top part of my hair off! My eyelashes were gone. My eyebrows were just little tiny black stubs that you could wipe* *away with your hands. <u>And all you could smell was the stench of singed hair!</u>*

The girls and I were the only ones at home at the time, and we were so relieved that I hadn't been killed that we burst out laughing. It really was funny how ridiculous I looked with this huge mountain of hair on top of my head and one big bald spot right in the front.

So I said to the kids, "I'll bet your dad doesn't even notice my hair." That's how bad things had gotten in our household! So we decided to play this game at the dinner table — "Don't say a word to Daddy about Mom's hair and see if he even notices." And do you know that Richard sat through that entire dinner and didn't notice my hair at all! I mean, there were little stubs of hair sticking out of my head, and he didn't even see it! **Now that's preoccupied!**

So the girls and I sat there, glancing back and forth at each other across the dinner table, until finally they started chuckling, and I couldn't hold it any longer. "Richard," I asked slowly, "do you notice anything different about me?" And my poor husband just stared straight at me and said, "No." Well, the girls and I burst into laughter.

"I blew the hair completely off the front of my head!" I exclaimed. "I have no eyelashes, no eyebrows!" But he just looked at me with a blank expression on his face and whispered, "Oh." That was when I knew how desperate things were. That was when I realized how far we had gone, how deep we had gotten, how dark it had become in our little household. Richard was still our wonderful, precious, loving husband and father, but he was totally preoccupied, eaten alive by this horrible mountain of debt. And that's when I told the Lord, **SOMETHING HAS GOT TO CHANGE!**

## I REFUSE TO PRESIDE OVER
## THE BIGGEST GARAGE SALE
## THE WORLD HAS EVER SEEN!

When that first disastrous summer drew to a close, I felt as if I had come to the end of the road. From one week to the next, we were barely making the payroll. Some of our creditors were literally pounding down our doors. Finally, I announced to our employees, "I will not be your leader through another summer like this one, *because the next cycle is always worse than the last one.* ***And I refuse to preside over the biggest garage sale the world has ever seen!***"

Then I would lie awake at night, tossing and turning, with the words Billy Graham spoke at ORU's dedication echoing in my spirit — "If this institution ever moves away from faith in the Bible, and faith in God, and putting God first, *then let us this day pronounce a curse on it.*" I was under a heavy charge from the Lord, and the weight of it was always upon me. I knew ORU was worth giving my life for, *but I felt as if I were living on the edge of a hurricane!*

It wasn't difficult for me to grasp why a man like King David would cry out, "Oh that I had wings like a dove; for then would I fly away!" (Psalm 55:6). *Friend, I desperately wanted a ticket out! I wanted to hop on an airplane and soar away to the farthest corner of the earth! Really, I wanted to just bury my head under the covers and never come out . . . BECAUSE I HAD NO INTENTION OF PRESIDING OVER THE DEATH OF MY DADDY'S DREAM!*

# Chapter 3

# IS THIS IT?

Now let me give you a word of warning before you read any further, because what you're about to read just may produce a spontaneous-combustion, Holy Ghost-filled *OUTPOURING* of joy and laughter which cannot be contained! I mean, you may not be able to drive a car for a while after reading this chapter. You may need to have a designated driver. You may not want to venture out in public too soon after reading this. *And you may want to warn your family about the hilariously happy side effects!*

You see, every place I've shared this testimony, there's been a tremendous uncontainable outbreak of holy joy and laughter like I've never seen before! So why don't you let me set the stage for you right now, and then you'll understand exactly what I'm talking about!

During that first grueling summer as President of ORU, I received an invitation from Pastor Karl Strader, a member of our ORU Board of Regents, to preach at Carpenter's Home Church in Lakeland, Florida. Now when I received that particular invitation, I had absolutely NO idea what God had in store for me.

I was so numb from the financial beating I was taking that I felt as if I were crawling around on my belly! I was almost oblivious to the world around me. Like so many Christians today, I was down in my spirit and hurting inside.

Before I boarded the plane for Lakeland, Lindsay

said to me, "Richard, something is going to happen to you while you're in Lakeland. You're going to turn a corner in your life and ministry!" But I just mumbled some kind of vague, halfhearted reply. Really, I didn't even have a glimmer of what she was talking about! *And, above all, I just wasn't impressed!*

Oh, I had heard the stories about the incredible revival of joy which had broken out in Brother Strader's church. I had heard about a young South African evangelist named Rodney Howard-Browne who had preached there and how the Spirit of God had swept over the crowds with indescribable joy and holy laughter!

According to the reports I had heard, this young man's ministry was very much like Brother Kenneth Hagin's ministry was when he was in his thirties — with a similar style and moving of the Spirit. And Brother Rodney's ministry was built solidly upon the Word of God, especially the Scripture in Nehemiah 8:10 which says, "The joy of the Lord is your strength."

Now before this evangelist had conducted a revival for Pastor Strader, Carpenter's Home Church had been ripped apart by a devastating church split, and they had also become strapped with overwhelming financial burdens. In fact, the Straders had almost lost the church.

But when Brother Rodney visited the Lakeland area, some five hundred churches cooperated in sponsoring the revival. Almost overnight, Carpenter's Home Church was jammed to the rafters with six thousand, seven thousand, eight thousand people packing the auditorium *at ten o'clock on Tuesday, Wednesday, and Thursday mornings!* And there were overflow crowds of nine thousand to ten thousand every night — six nights a week — FOR EIGHT WEEKS!

I had heard Pastor Strader describe in vivid detail how he would find himself sprawled on the floor of the church night after night, laughing hysterically in the Spirit. *And God began to pour out a fresh baptism of holy joy and laughter on the entire Lakeland area!*

At one point during that unprecedented revival, they set up a portable swimming pool beside the altar, and some two thousand people were baptized in it! **It was the most earthshaking, Heaven-moving outpouring of God ever seen in the city of Lakeland!**

Now there's one particular story that stands out in my mind from those amazing Holy Ghost services in Lakeland.

One night there was a woman in the congregation who had to work the late shift on her job that night. So she slipped out of the auditorium, climbed into her car, and set out on her drive to work.

**But all at once she made a terrible mistake.** Halfway there, she flipped on the radio and tuned in to the station which was broadcasting the revival. As soon as she heard that Holy Ghost laughter streaming across the airwaves, she became so drunk in the Spirit that she started weaving all over the highway!

Just at that instant, a motorcycle officer with the Florida Highway Patrol spotted her and pulled her over. Then that poor unsuspecting man walked up to the door of her car and started to write out a ticket. By then she was absolutely shrieking with laughter, and the radio was still blaring. "What are you listening to?" the officer asked her with a puzzled look on his face. Suddenly, she became as sober as a church mouse and started telling him all about the revival. <u>And he was all ears</u>!

In the next split second, the officer fell to the ground, laughing uncontrollably in the Spirit! So the woman got out of her car and helped him to his feet. When he could finally contain himself, he told her, "I've been running from God for fifteen years!" *And she led that man to Jesus right there beside her car!*

## THE JOY OF THE LORD GOT ALL OVER ME MORE THAN ANYPLACE ELSE!

I knew from all the reports I was hearing that this revival of Holy Ghost joy was real! I knew it was an out-and-out sovereign move of God's Spirit, *but I just wasn't interested.* Really, it wasn't on my agenda. After all, I had the weight of the whole ORU debt resting on me personally. *I was in no frame of mind to laugh!*

Now I had grown up in certain circles where people did unusual things according to the world's standards. I mean, they marched up and down the aisles of the church in a Jericho victory march before the Lord. They sang and shouted and clapped their hands and made a joyful noise unto God, shaking the rafters with the sound of their praise!

So I wasn't opposed in any way to what was happening in Pastor Strader's church, <u>but I was a person who was **usually** in control</u>. I planned to go to Lakeland as scheduled, and I would have my time of ministry there. Then I would board a flight for Tulsa, fly back home, *AND THAT WOULD BE THAT!*

I wasn't the least bit startled when Pastor Strader warned me, "Richard, no one has been able to do very much preaching in our church since this revival broke out. Everyone who has visited here has been overtaken by Holy Ghost joy and laughter!"

Then he went on to describe a minister whom I've known for more than twenty years who had tried to preach there a few weeks earlier. According to Pastor Strader, when that man stepped onto the platform, his legs immediately buckled beneath him, sending him sprawling onto the floor. *And then he just lay there for a solid hour, convulsing with hysterical laughter!*

Now I knew it wasn't like this particular individual to act that way, but I was so numb from the problems I was grappling with that I mumbled, "Well, okay, so what?" I couldn't picture myself falling on the floor laughing! *Happy, hilarious laughter was the farthest thing in the world from my mind!*

Friend, when the joy of the Lord came into my life, IT CAME UPON ME SUDDENLY. I didn't have the faintest idea that God was about to send His holy joy and laughter raining down on me from Heaven! **If you want to know the real truth of the matter, I was totally put out and disgusted with life!**

So when I stepped onto the platform at Carpenter's Home Church, I started singing and then immediately launched into my sermon, which I titled, "How to Get Out of Your Present Mess." Really, my message was based upon my own agonizing struggle to break free from the financial mess at ORU!

I was preaching my heart out when, all at once, the Lord gave me a word of knowledge about someone's ear being healed. So I called a man out of the crowd, and then God impressed me to lay my hands on him. The instant I touched that man, he started falling to the floor under the power of God. *And suddenly the realization flashed through my mind that no one was there to catch him!*

Now I was holding a microphone in one hand, so I reached around behind him with my other hand to try to catch him. He was a big man, and the force of his fall sent me sailing through the air right over the top of his head! I mean, I turned a full somersault over that man's body and landed on my feet on the other side!

It was a Holy Ghost somersault! I looked like one of those gymnasts in the Olympics. And, believe me, IT WAS FUNNY! You know — ha-ha, the evangelist turned a somersault in church! ***And the whole congregation roared with laughter!***

But about twenty minutes later, they were still laughing, and it just wasn't funny anymore! I looked around that auditorium in amazement as great waves of laughter swept over the crowd. I could see big tears rolling down people's faces, and some people were even falling onto the floor, laughing uncontrollably. Everywhere I looked, all I could see were "holy rollers"!

Pastor Strader was laughing so hard that his face was literally streaked with tears. His son Steven, who is an ORU graduate, was down on his hands and knees, pounding the floor with his fists, laughing hysterically. It looked like everyone in the whole church was laughing!

After a few minutes, I glanced over at the pastor and asked him sheepishly, "What is this?"

He said, "This is it!"

I said, "What's it?"

He said, "This!"

Now remember, I had been almost completely without any type of joy or laughter for many months because of the trials I was going through. So when I started laughing that day, it was because that Holy Ghost somersault was funny.

But all of a sudden, I began to feel the strangest sensation welling up in my belly. It was like a rumbling sensation. I felt something very peculiar bubbling up inside me! It was the same kind of feeling I have when I pray in tongues, but this time I felt laughter flowing up out of my innermost being. **And I began to laugh when there was no earthly reason to laugh!**

It wasn't a chest laugh, a surface laugh, but rather it was laughter that was rolling up from way down deep in my soul. *It was joy! It was holy! It was holy laughter! And it could not be contained!*

All at once, the Scripture in John 7:38 came flooding up in my spirit. It's the passage where Jesus declared, "Out of [your] belly shall flow rivers of living water." And then the Gospel writer goes on to say that He was speaking of the Holy Ghost, which had not yet been given because Jesus had not yet been glorified.

Friend, when the joy of the Lord hit my life, it hit me like a streak of lightning, and I began to laugh from my belly area in much the same way that I pray in tongues from my belly area! Now up until that point, about the only spark of relief I could get from all the hair-raising struggles in my life was

37

by praying in tongues. *But, all at once, this holy joy and laughter was giving me a relief from my heartaches like I'd never known before!*

I promptly forgot the rest of my sermon and collapsed on the front row of the church, doubled over with Holy Ghost laughter. I was so far gone that I just laid my head down on the lap of the lady next to me, *laughing in the Spirit with reckless abandon!* I tell you, the joy of the Lord got all over me more than anyplace else, *AND I NEEDED IT SO DESPERATELY!*

The more I laughed, the more I felt my burdens being stripped away. I felt the fear evaporate, the pressure lighten, and the terrible mind-boggling stress just take wing and fly away!

There was a total rejuvenation of my spirit, soul, and body! I felt as if my entire being had been infused with divine energy from Heaven! Now my troubles hadn't changed one bit, <u>BUT I HAD CHANGED</u>! **Something remarkable had happened to me!**

No one took control of the service that day at Carpenter's Home Church, because no one <u>could</u> take control. And yet while we were laughing, the Spirit of the Lord swept through that auditorium as hundreds of people flocked to the altar. Healings, miracles, and salvations were breaking loose so quickly that I could scarcely believe my eyes! In a moment's time, the whole place erupted with the healing power of Jesus! *And before that service was over, we were ENGULFED with a mighty stream of miracles from the Lord!*

# 'FOR THE BENEFIT OF THE RADIO AUDIENCE, OUR EVANGELIST IS ON THE FLOOR!'

Later that day, I was burning up the phone lines back to Tulsa, trying to explain to my wife, Lindsay, the astonishing things that had happened to me. "I knew it!" she exclaimed as she rejoiced with me over the telephone. "I knew you were going to turn a corner in your life!" Then she added, *"Bring it back home to Tulsa! Bring it back to ORU!"*

For the rest of the afternoon, Pastor Strader tried to explain to me what this baptism of joy was all about, but I still couldn't grasp it. When we arrived at the service that night, the instant he introduced me, I slid right out of my chair onto the floor, **AND I COULDN'T GET UP!** *I was laughing hysterically in the Spirit!*

I felt like such a fool! I mean, you go to church and just fall out of your chair laughing? For about ten minutes I was sprawled out on the floor, laughing uncontrollably, *and nothing whatsoever was funny!* Brother Strader was trying to carry on the service, while I was lying in a heap on the front row of the church, howling with laughter! I tried to move, but I couldn't budge. It was as if I were nailed to the floor! *My body felt as if it weighed a thousand pounds!*

Now anyone who knows me very well knows that I'm not the type of person who just collapses on the floor, rolls around, and shrieks with laughter! I'm much too respectable, too dignified, for that! My wife says that I'm very detailed, very methodical. Really, she says that I'm almost stuffy! I go to bed at night with my pajamas creased, and they're still creased in the morning when I crawl out of bed, and every hair on my head is still in place!

Well, the service was on the radio live that night, so Brother Strader announced, "For the benefit of the radio audience, our evangelist is on the floor!" Then he had to kill some time until I could regain my composure!

For the next few minutes, he described in vivid detail how God had poured out a fresh baptism of joy in his life during Brother Rodney Howard-Browne's revival. "I kind of had a permanent spot right down there on the floor where I seemed to wind up every night!" he exclaimed laughingly. "One night my ushers traced a human outline on that spot, and they wrote on it, *Reserved for Pastor!*"

After Brother Strader had covered for me for fifteen or twenty minutes, I finally managed to struggle to my feet. But the instant I hit the platform, somebody yelled, "Sing!"

"You've got to be kidding!" I gasped. "I can't sing!" *But I had them go ahead and roll the soundtrack!* I got out only about two or three bars of the song before I slumped down onto the platform, shaking with laughter all over again!

By that time, the entire congregation was roaring! One man was down on the floor in the aisle on his stomach, laughing and wildly flapping his arms in the air! All I had to do was take one look at him, *and I was gone!* I must have laughed **nonstop** for thirty more minutes!

As waves of Holy Ghost laughter rippled across that auditorium, *suddenly the gifts of the Spirit began to flow.* One young woman who had suffered for eight years from a horrible ringing or roaring sound in her ears was perfectly healed by the Lord. I never even touched her. *All I did was spit on her!* <u>Not intentionally, of course!</u> When she came up to give her testimony, I got tickled and burst out laughing in the Spirit, and I accidentally showered her with spit!

Friend, what happened to me that weekend in Lakeland, Florida, was nothing short of a flat-out sovereign move of God! And once I yielded to the Lord, I became so immersed in His presence that I began to cast myself aside, saying, "Lord, if this is of You, then I must decrease and You must increase. God, I'm putting my life into Your hands!"

A very soul-stirring word of prophecy came forth that night from a dear man in the audience. He said to me, *Richard, I got very emotional when I heard you say you wanted God to give you a fresh anointing. And I'm here to tell you that He has given you that fresh anointing — an anointing of joy — to take back with you to bless your ministry, to bless you as president of that university.*

*I am so in awe of the fact that your dad was a stammering, stuttering person who stood in the middle of an empty field and God placed that [calling] on him. And now the mantle is being handed down, and it's going to be a different kind of anointing. It's going to be an anointing of joy and prosperity on that campus like never before!*

*Brother, I am telling you, <u>you are a different person</u>. God is changing you. Your countenance, your demeanor, is different. People look to you to be this awesome leader, but here you are strewn out on the floor [under the power of the Lord], <u>and I'm impressed with that . . . because you're willing to submit to the move of the Holy Spirit!</u>* **And that's what He's** *looking for — a willingness to let go and let God be God!*

## WHO IS THIS NUT SITTING NEXT TO ME?

When I boarded my flight for Tulsa the next morning, I had a copy of a brand-new best-seller which I wanted to read. So I was just sitting there, minding my own business, completely engrossed in this gripping novel when, out of the blue, I burst into sidesplitting laughter right there on the plane!

Well, the person next to me was so startled that he glanced over in my direction, wide-eyed, and started peeking over at the cover of my book to see what on earth I was reading. When it finally dawned on him that I was reading a high-powered action thriller, he looked at me as if to say, *Who is this nut sitting next to me?*

It was only a few moments later when the flight attendant leaned over and whispered, "Is anything wrong?"

"No," I told her between gasps of laughter, *and I just kept right on laughing!* There I was, reading a spine-tingling book, and I was absolutely roaring! Of course, by then, the man next to me was certain that it was time to send for the straitjacket!

In fact, all the people in my entire section of the plane kept staring at me, but I couldn't have cared less! By the time I had laughed for about ten minutes straight, some of those passengers couldn't control themselves any longer, and they were laughing with me! Why? ***Because laughter is contagious!***

When I landed in Tulsa, I could hardly wait for

Lindsay to watch the video of those incredible services at Carpenter's Home Church. I wanted her to see her dignified husband rolling around on the floor, laughing hysterically in the Spirit! So I've asked her to describe in her own words her reaction the very first time we watched that exciting video:

*Richard had tried to explain to me over the telephone what had happened to him in Lakeland, but there was just no way! Finally, he said, "I'm going to bring it home on video!" So that first night, we stayed up all night and watched that two-hour video THREE TIMES! That amounts to six hours of laughing in the Spirit!*

*I'll tell you what — a merry heart did good like a medicine for us that night! We took our Holy Ghost medicine, and we were happy campers!* ***And we had*** ***no reason in the natural to be happy!***

*When I watched the joy of the Lord hit my Richard, I saw Mr. Perfect turn a somersault in midair and roll head over heels on the floor of the church! I mean, here's a man who is usually in control. He goes to sleep in one position, and he's still in the same position the next morning. He wakes up every morning with his pajamas still creased, every hair in place.* ***It's disgusting!***

*But as I watched that video, I saw Mr. Perfect totally lose control!* ***It was the most glorious thing*** ***I'd ever seen!*** *I remember watching that precious young lady who was telling him a tragic story about a very serious hearing problem she had experienced. Right in the middle of what she was saying, the joy hit Richard, and it hit her, and he was laughing so hard that he actually spit in her face! I tell you, that's just not like my husband! But that woman had been miraculously healed by the power of God!*

*All of these years I've seen Richard walk by faith, speak by faith, live by faith. He's a person who has been totally stable in every area of his life. He doesn't ordinarily have high highs or low lows. But because of the troubles we were facing at ORU, every time we were struck by another problem, I would see it overwhelm and consume him.*

*But after the joy of the Lord came into his life, his entire personality changed! Now, when a problem comes, he isn't consumed by it. <u>Instead, he is consumed by the Answer — Jesus Christ!</u> He is consumed with the joy of the Lord! No matter what comes at him from the right or the left, from the North, South, East, or West, he just handles it by faith **and Holy Ghost joy! <u>Really, he has become a new man because of it!</u>***

*When the joy hit Richard's life, ORU'S TROUBLES DIDN'T CHANGE OVERNIGHT. What changed was Richard's inner man. It was the first time I had seen him have such a deep inner peace and such overflowing joy RIGHT IN THE MIDDLE OF SOME OF THE MOST HORRIBLE DEPRESSING TRIALS THAT WE HAD EVER GONE THROUGH!*

*I'm not talking about an emotional outburst — ha-ha-ha, tee-hee-hee — and when the next problem hits, you're dying on the inside! <u>No, God is allowing Richard to see the problems in a different light.</u> AND THAT HAS MADE A BIG CHANGE IN HIM!*

*Isn't it amazing how you can get down to the rock bottom of life and wonder, "Does God even know where I am?" **Friend, He knows.** And He knew that Richard wasn't going to make it without the joy of the Lord to strengthen him and lift his spirit.*

*We've always had a happy home and a happy*

*marriage, but today our home is a joy-filled, hilariously happy home! The laughter at our house is contagious, and a merry heart has kept us through all the fiery trials and ordeals that we've faced!*

*If you've been skeptical about the joy of the Lord, if you think it's some kind of hocus-pocus, all I can tell you is that I saw the joy of the Lord hit my husband — hit his mind, his heart, but more than anything else, hit his spirit. And when it hit his spirit, he came home to me a new man.* **I had my Richard back. I SAW MY HUSBAND COMPLETELY, 100 PERCENT, RESTORED BY THE JOY OF THE LORD!**

## YOU MAY NEED GOD TO HELP YOU PUT YOUR WORRIER ON THE BACK BURNER!

This wasn't some kind of crazy, slapstick comedy adventure which I experienced on my trip to Lakeland, Florida. You see, while I was laughing, chains were being broken in the spirit realm. I felt the load lighten. I felt the dark clouds lift. I felt as if I could fly! *All of those awful burdens suddenly began to roll away!*

Now I'm not saying those things weren't important anymore, but they no longer had a vise-like grip on me. It was as if God had put all of my worrying on the back burner! **And you may need God to help you put your worrier on the back burner too!**

When that mighty torrent of Holy Ghost joy came rushing through my life, I HAD TO HAVE IT. It was as if I had been out on the windblown sands of the desert for days, under the hot, boiling sun. I don't believe I could have staggered one more step through that barren wasteland if God hadn't come down and lifted the load.

But when this joy-filled worship began rolling out of my spirit, suddenly I began to change. The stress began to melt away, and the ulcer I had developed was healed. Now, I have a **knowing** in my heart, not a **gnawing** in the pit of my stomach! There's a brand-new freedom in my soul that I've never had before! And the more I laugh, the more I get into the rhythm of God's Holy Ghost blessings! *THE LORD IS REVOLUTIONIZING MY LIFE THROUGH THIS MIGHTY BAPTISM OF JOY!*

# Chapter 4

# ORAL ROBERTS UNIVERSITY ERUPTS WITH A REVIVAL OF HOLY GHOST JOY!

Can you imagine the thoughts that raced through my mind when I arrived back in Tulsa from Lakeland and heard that Rodney Howard-Browne was going to conduct a revival at Rhema Bible Training Center, *just a few short miles from the Oral Roberts University campus?*

By that time, I had a very strong desire to invite Brother Rodney to minister at ORU. I wanted our students, faculty, and staff to experience a spontaneous, uncontrollable tidal wave of joy and laughter just as I had! So my dad and mother and Lindsay and I decided to attend several of those services, which were hosted by our dear friends, Dr. and Mrs. Kenneth E. Hagin, Sr., and the Reverend and Mrs. Kenneth Hagin, Jr.

Night after night, Lindsay and I wound up spending much of the evening ON THE FLOOR LAUGHING! I remember one particular service when she and I fell out of our pew, sprawled on the floor, <u>and ended up directly underneath Brother and Sister Hagin's pew as the joy of the Lord flooded our lives</u>!

Another night, Brother Rodney called me up to the platform to give a testimony, and I began by saying, "Well, we've had a $42-million debt," *but those were the only words I managed to blurt out!*

The next thing I knew, I had collapsed right there on the floor, laughing so hard that it felt as if my sides would split open! While I was lying there, I heard the Holy Spirit speaking in my spirit, "In the same way that you're laughing here tonight, you're going to laugh while I pay off your $42-million debt!" *Oh, those words meant EVERYTHING to me!*

By the time I managed to wobble back to my seat, Lindsay had draped herself across the pew, laughing. "What's all that?" I asked when I saw a huge puddle of spit. "I spit all over the pew!" she said, and then she burst out laughing all over again! Now if I'd had any doubts about whether the joy was real, that put an end to it right there! *Because that's just not Lindsay's speed.* I mean, my wife is really respectable! **She's a dignified lady!**

And speaking of dignified ladies, I'll never forget as long as I live the night my mother, Evelyn Roberts, and Brother Hagin's wife, Oretha, were laughing so hard in the Spirit that they were stumbling and falling down, absolutely drunk in the Holy Ghost. Friend, those are two of the most refined, most ladylike women of God I have ever met. But they were having such a hallelujah time that night that they were falling on top of each other, creating a hilarious traffic jam in the hallway of Rhema Bible Church!

As they staggered out of the building that night, they looked like two drunk ladies trying to make their way home after an all-night drinking spree. *But I knew they hadn't been drinking alcohol. THEY HAD BEEN DRINKING FROM THOSE RIVERS OF LIVING WATER THAT JESUS TALKED ABOUT IN JOHN 7:38. THEY WERE BURSTING WITH HOLY*

## *GHOST LAUGHTER AND JOY!*

My mother told me later, "Richard, when I was a young girl, we were in Pentecostal services where the power of God was so strong that many could not walk home when the service was over. Many just fell onto the floor laughing, and some had to be carried home in carts."

That's when it dawned on me that there had to be a reason why Peter stood up on the Day of Pentecost and announced to the crowd, "These men aren't drunk on alcohol as you suppose they are" (see Acts 2:15). Now when drunks are staggering home from the neighborhood bar, they aren't speaking in tongues and prophesying, are they? I mean, those men must have been doing something besides speaking in a heavenly prayer language or Peter wouldn't have had to stand up before that whole assembly and declare that they weren't drunk on alcohol!

What on earth do you suppose they were doing? Could they have been stumbling down the street, hilariously drunk in the Spirit? Or perhaps they were laughing and slapping each other on the back or slurring their words when they talked. Perhaps they were slipping off the curb or tripping over their own feet. Whatever it was, it must have been something that made them appear to be drunk on alcohol. But Peter boldly proclaimed, "They're not drunk on alcohol!" NO! THEY WERE DRUNK ON THE NEW WINE OF THE SPIRIT!

### BROTHER RODNEY TOLD THE LORD, "THIS LAUGHTER IS RUINING MY MINISTRY!"

I remember one night during that unforgettable

revival when the spirit of prophecy began flowing through my father. His spirit locked with Brother Rodney's spirit as the Lord gave my father a powerful anointed word for that young man. There was such a binding in the Lord among the three of us that night, but what really got ahold of me was the way Brother Rodney made the Word of God leap off the pages of the Bible! **And, friend, I was looking for the preaching of the Word!**

Later I asked Brother Rodney the question, "How did this new move of the Spirit start?"

He replied, "Richard, I didn't want it to start. All of a sudden, this Holy Ghost laughter began happening in my meetings, and I was very irritated and upset by it. It was hard to preach because people were laughing and falling under the power of God. So I told the Lord, 'This laughter is ruining my ministry!' And He said to me, 'Your ministry needs to be ruined!' Then God added, 'I've seen your ministry. **Now let Me show you Mine.'"**

That fall I invited Brother Rodney Howard-Browne for a Holy Ghost revival at Oral Roberts University, and I shut down the entire campus for two whole days. You see, I wanted all of our faculty, staff, and students to experience an earthshaking, Heaven-moving encounter with God!

Now I didn't invite Brother Rodney to ORU so he could teach us how to laugh. Nobody needs to LEARN how to laugh. Brother Rodney doesn't have a "laughing" ministry and neither do I! He has been mislabeled as the "laughing preacher," but really, *he is not a humorous person at all!*

When Rodney Howard-Browne arrived on the campus of Oral Roberts University, he began preaching like a man from another world! You talk about delivering the Word of God! **He poured out Scripture after Scripture on the subject of Bible joy.** The atmosphere was absolutely electrified as he preached about the outpouring of the Spirit on the Day of Pentecost. *And then he said that God had shown him that the church has lost its joy. Somehow the body of Christ has forgotten that the joy of the Lord is their strength.*

He described in vivid detail the mighty revivals from the Day of Pentecost through the present day. We were literally spellbound, sitting on the edges of our seats, as he told about the early revivals which swept like wildfire across the American frontier.

He gave thrilling accounts of the Kentucky outpouring of June 1800, when it's reported that the move of the Spirit was so overpowering that the floor was strewn with the bodies of people who had fallen under the power! One observer said that when the Spirit of the Lord fell, some people began to jerk, while others danced, wept, **laughed,** ran, shouted, and sang beautiful heavenly songs unto the Lord. *Let me tell you, our forefathers knew how to have a real, heartfelt Holy Ghost revival!*

Brother Rodney also related that in many of the meetings of Charles Finney, the great revivalist, people would suddenly begin to wail at the top of their lungs. During one particular service, Brother Finney reportedly shouted to the crowd, "Be quiet! You're not in hell yet!" But they just wouldn't be quiet!

Finally, they had wailed so long and so loudly that Brother Finney walked over to an empty fireplace, stuck his head inside, and covered his mouth with a handkerchief *because he was laughing uncontrollably with an indescribable joy!* **And that's the way many of his mighty revivals would break out!**

Brother Rodney also described how in the days of John Wesley's famous camp meetings, the horses would often come under the power of the Lord, and they would gallop for many miles at breakneck speed, ***taking their riders directly to the camp meeting!***

As Brother Rodney painted a picture of those early Holy Ghost revivals, my mind was suddenly flooded with memories of the stories my dad had told me about services when he was a boy. And scenes began to flash through my mind from some of Brother Hagin's meetings when as many as ten thousand people would break into spontaneous Holy Ghost laughter — and nothing at all was funny!

It wasn't a question of laughing because something was funny. It was a question of uproarious, joy-filled laughter — *laughter which simply could not be contained!* It just kind of got all over you and started bursting out the seams! **And the more you laughed, THE MORE YOU LAUGHED!**

Brother Rodney proclaimed, *This is not new! It might be new to you, but it's not new. It has been around as long as the Holy Ghost has been around. Whenever the Holy Ghost walks in the door, there's going to be an upheaval. Whenever the Holy Ghost walks in the door, man loses control and God takes control.*

*You can come down, you can roll on the floor, you can be carried out, but if you don't allow the Holy Ghost to change you, you're going to stay the same as you ever were! You've got to allow the Spirit of God to do a work deep within your heart. If you don't allow the Holy Ghost to . . . change you, you are nothing more than a clanging cymbal and a noisy gong!*

Brother Rodney stressed, above all, that no revival, no outpouring of the Spirit, should be judged by its outward manifestations. IT MUST BE JUDGED BY ITS FRUIT! He declared, *What is the fruit of . . . people's lives when they come out of that encounter with God? If they're not a better person, then I question whether or not it is of God.*

As Brother Rodney boldly proclaimed the Word of God, a mighty baptism of joy seemed to leap across the auditorium. All of a sudden, great waves of holy joy and laughter swept over the crowd! At the close of one of the services, he asked the ORU students, "How many of you want me to lay hands on you for God to give you a fresh touch of the joy of the Lord?" Virtually every hand flew up in the air!

So Brother Rodney began making his way through the huge crowd of students filling the aisles, laying hands on them until there was no place left to minister to them! Many slumped to the floor under the power of God, while others rolled around on the carpet, laughing uproariously in the Spirit! Christ's Chapel was jammed with the bodies of the students — in the aisles, out in the lobby areas, in the hallways — *and there were still close to two thousand more who were clamoring to be prayed for!*

Brother Rodney's brother (who was traveling with him at the time) asked me, "What shall we do?" So I suggested that we take the rest of the students outside onto the grass. It was a warm, breezy fall day, and that was the biggest empty spot we had close by. So we reorganized the prayer line outdoors on the grass!

The bodies of the students were strewn all over the lawn that day! I mean, the news media would have had a field day if they had flown over ORU in a helicopter! People were beating the ground with their fists, kicking their feet in the air, laughing hilariously in the Spirit, and rolling around with the bugs on the grass!

I recall after one particular service, our daughter Jordan, who was nine years old at the time, laughed and cackled and prayed in tongues continuously for an hour and forty-five minutes. She couldn't get out a single word of English!

When we got her home that night, we tried to put her to bed, but every time we tucked her into bed, she slid right out again, laughing uncontrollably in the Spirit! ***Believe me, you can't get a nine-year-old to fake something like that!***

Finally, after about four tries, Lindsay suggested, "Let's put her into a tub of warm water and see if we can get her to relax." So we put her into some warm bathwater, and after a while we got her to sleep in bed!

During another one of those same revival services, there was a precious little five-year-old girl who just stood there trembling, absolutely still, with a little smile on her face and a tear trickling down her cheek, for forty-five minutes! I'm talking about a five-year-old here! **She never moved a muscle for forty-five minutes!**

I remember very vividly the service when our middle daughter, Olivia, who was six at the time, was literally glued to the floor in the holy presence of God. While she was lying in the aisle, one of her little friends was rolling around next to her, hilariously filled with holy joy and laughter!

After the service was over, those two little girls looked up at Lindsay, wide-eyed, and exclaimed excitedly, *"That was fun!"* **I tell you, children need to see that church can be fun again! They desperately need to know that Jesus Christ is fun!**

## FOLKS, THIS REVIVAL HAS CHANGED ME!

As the revival drew to a close, Brother Rodney asked the question, "Who has been touched by the power of God during these services?" Hands shot up in the air all over the place, and a number of students came forward to give their testimonies. Here are just a few of the highlights:

One young man reported: *When Chancellor Oral Roberts stepped out in front of everybody, and I saw the joy of the Lord hit him, I fell out laughing. I was so full of joy that I ran outside and wrapped my arms around a tree and slowly sank to the ground. Then I started weeping.*

*You see, my mother and father have been divorced since I was two years old, and my father and I never had a real father-and-son relationship. All those years I hated my father. It was as if I had a grudge against him.*

*While I was hugging that tree, I suddenly felt this little boy inside me, who was hurting, crying for his father, come out of me. And I felt as if, for the first time in my life, I could be reconciled to my father!* **That same young man appeared as a guest on our TV program a few months later and reported that**

**he and his father reconciled for the first time in all those years!**

A young theology student from a noncharismatic denomination told us this soul-searching story: *I'm a senior here at ORU, and I've had four years of practicing being a cynic. I came to this meeting today thinking, "I'm going to see heresy."*

*Now I've never believed in speaking in tongues before, but when Brother Rodney gave the altar call, I knew it was time for me to rededicate my life to Christ. So we went back to the prayer room, and all of a sudden, these strange words that I didn't understand started coming out of my mouth.*

*All day long I've been happy. I've been excited. If you're a cynic, you couldn't be any more cynical than I was. I've seen it all. But this is real!* ___**Folks, this revival has changed me!**___

After our fall break, we received another heart-touching testimony from an ORU student who took this revival of holy joy and laughter back home with him to New York City. His pastor had already heard about the outbreak of Holy Ghost joy at ORU, so he invited the student to testify during the Sunday morning service.

When that young man opened his mouth to talk about the ORU revival, his pastor fell under the power of God, laughing uncontrollably in the Spirit. Then the whole church broke out into spontaneous holy joy and laughter! Friend, they had a hallelujah Holy Ghost blowout that Sunday, and the service continued until the middle of the afternoon!

Now this young man and his mother and sister were all Bible-believing Christians. But his father was a hardened atheist, a man who adamantly insisted, "I'll take Muhammed, I'll take Buddha, but I won't take Jesus!"

Well, by the time they got home from church that afternoon, his father was pacing back and forth, boiling mad because his wife hadn't gotten home in time to cook his Sunday dinner! After this young man started giving him a blow-by-blow description of this fresh outpouring of Holy Ghost joy, all of a sudden his father fell on the floor and began laughing hysterically in the Spirit.

When the man could finally contain himself, he blurted out, "I don't know what this is, **but I want it!"**

His son replied, "Dad, you've got to get saved!" ***AND HE LED HIS FATHER TO JESUS RIGHT THERE ON THE SPOT!***

## WHAT'S THE BOTTOM LINE?

At the end of that first day of revival at ORU, I went home and crawled into bed, *but my mind was still spinning.* All at once, I got terribly worried. I cried out to the Lord, ***There's got to be something more than the laughter, or this revival is going to be greatly misunderstood!***

You see, I'm a person who's always looking for the bottom line. I want to zero in on the net results. I'm not ashamed of falling under the power of God or being overtaken with happy, hilarious Holy Ghost joy! But what I want to know is, ***What do you do with your life after you're filled with the joy of the Lord?***

The next day when that young man poured out his heart about the hurt little boy inside him being healed, the whole place literally broke up. All at once our laughter turned to brokenness and weeping before the Lord, and a rush of the Spirit flooded through my heart when I realized that it wasn't just laughter for laughter's sake! There was a very potent bottom line to the laughter.

> ## And the bottom line is a life that's changed by the joy of the Lord!

I tell you, we had a humdinger of a revival at Oral Roberts University that fall! The miracles were so evident, along with the joy of the Lord and holy pandemonium all over the campus! There was weeping and a true, heartfelt repentance before the Lord as some of the students accepted Jesus as their personal Savior, and many drew closer to the Lord! It was a good old-fashioned *OUTPOURING* of the Holy Ghost and fire!

A brand-new liveliness, a freshness, a spark of revival and holy joy has swept across our campus. Unprecedented things are happening! *GOD IS REVOLUTIONIZING ORAL ROBERTS UNIVERSITY THROUGH THIS AMAZING NEW OUTBREAK OF JOY!*

# Chapter 5

# MY ASSOCIATES
# THOUGHT IT WAS TIME
# TO SEND
# FOR THE STRAITJACKET!

When you're the founder of a world-class university such as Oral Roberts University, and you've raised it up out of the ground with your bare hands as my dad did, *in many ways you come to grips with its operation by osmosis!* But when you arrive on the scene as the second generation like I did, you've got to dive down into the trenches and learn from the ground up. *You've got to discover for yourself exactly what makes a university tick!*

Over the past few years, I've immersed myself in the inner workings of ORU, getting hands-on experience in every aspect of its operation. In some ways, not knowing how to operate a university was really a blessing. *I just forged ahead in faith, tackling each new obstacle in my own way as God led me!*

Every morning I gathered the various department heads and the leaders of the university and ministry around a conference table. And while the pages before us were blank, we put our heads and hearts together and allowed God to show us how to run His university.

There was an openness, an honesty, and an unusual camaraderie among us. There was no personal "kingdom building." We all labored together for the common good, and we were deadly serious about

59

making it through the rough financial waters **with all of our cargo intact!**

Every morning when we received word about the income for that day, we would face the grim task of deciding how to dole out the meager payments to our creditors. There were times when so little money was trickling in that our business meetings turned into Holy Ghost prayer meetings, *because there was just no money to pay the mushrooming pile of bills!*

So when I returned from that remarkable life-changing trip to Lakeland, Florida, I gathered my associates together and gave them a full report of what had happened to me. Well, they just stared at me in stunned disbelief. You could see their minds turning, as if to say, *Richard, you've always been so balanced, but now you've gone off the deep end!*

They looked at me like I was crazy! *You know, a few bricks short of a load. The lights are on, but nobody's home!* I'm sure they were wondering if the pressure had simply become too much for me. ***Really, they looked as though they thought it was time to send for a straitjacket!***

But now they've seen firsthand the spiritual revolution and the dramatic changes the joy of the Lord has brought into my life. AND THEY KNOW THE JOY IS REAL! So I've asked several members of my Administrative Council to tell you in their own words exactly how this tidal wave of joy has impacted their lives as well as mine!

## I SAW A NEW SPIRITUAL POWER COMING THROUGH HIM!

*It's almost impossible to describe the conditions*

*under which Richard entered into the presidency of Oral Roberts University. The financial crises that had hit ministries across this nation had taken their toll on this ministry and also ORU.*

*We were $42 million in debt, with no plans for repayment and not enough money for daily operations, going further into debt every day. Almost weekly, Richard had to decide what to cut next in order to survive — whether it was cancelling an academic program, or taking the TV program off another television station, or a multitude of other things.*

*All the buildings on campus needed repairs and renovations, especially the students' dormitories. The library even needed library books! The number of employees had to be cut, and those who remained absorbed more responsibilities with no hope of receiving any raises. Creditors were pounding on our door, some threatening lawsuits. Some vendors were sticking by us, while others refused to service us. There were needs in all areas of the university and ministry.*

*On top of all this heavy responsibility, I saw Richard maintain, and even increase, a heavy travel schedule, going to churches and cities to preach and pray for people in need, while he continued taping television programs and corresponding with the Partners of the ministry.*

*Soon after this, Richard formed a special committee, a management team, to meet with him every morning concerning these seemingly impossible situations. So many days it seemed there was no way we were going to financially make it through another day! At times I thought we would all burst — one might describe it as walking through hell together. We held on only by our faith in God and our integrity before*

*Him.*

*We could tell the tension was increasing as the load of responsibilities was mounting on Richard. It was like watching a rubber band being pulled tighter and tighter. We wondered how much more he could take without breaking. One of two things had to happen — he would either come through this with his faith tried like gold and be the leader God had ordained, or he would crumble under the load and be buried with all that he had fought for. Something had to give, or should I say, <u>Someone</u> had to give <u>something</u>.*

*When I first heard that Richard had had an experience with joy and laughing "in the Spirit" at Karl Strader's church, I wondered how this was going to affect someone who had such <u>serious</u> responsibilities as he. What I saw was totally different from what I expected!*

*First of all, I saw a new spiritual POWER coming through him. Most of us don't think of power when we think of joy and laughter. In fact, we usually think of someone as not having much responsibility in life if they have time to laugh and have joy. But through joy, Richard was filled with a spiritual power that I believe has enabled him to withstand the worst of financial news (which was given to him often) and to make extremely difficult decisions with faith and wisdom and still remain concerned about others around him while he was going through tough times.*

*The most unusual display of this joy I now see in Richard's life is in the <u>increase</u> of healing miracles that God performs through his ministry. His words of knowledge given during services are very accurate and produce such tremendous results! People with all kinds of ailments, sicknesses, and physical problems* *are frequently healed right on the spot as he gives words of knowledge from God concerning their exact conditions.*

*After this joy came into Richard's life, I can remember when he called the management team together for a special meeting, and he read II Chronicles 20 to us about how King Jehoshaphat and the Israelites were facing impossible odds with an enemy army. God instructed them not to fear or be dismayed because the battle was the Lord's!*

*Then Jehoshaphat sent out the praise team in front of the soldiers, and as they marched and praised God, God destroyed the enemy! It took the children of Israel three days to carry away all the spoils of the enemy because they were so great! And God gave them rest in the land.*

*After Richard read that passage, he told us that he wanted no doubters on the committee, and no fear and no dismay. He wanted us to come into a unity of faith with him as the leader. Since that time, we have seen miracle after miracle after miracle. When we have been at the point of closing the doors because we were out of money, God has always come through with a financial miracle.*

*I remember once when we were concerned about paying the past-due debt, we all came into an agreement that if God would provide large lump sums of money, we would put as much of it as possible toward the past-due debt. In the next few days, we received a check for $1 million! And we paid off some past-due debts!*

*One time when Richard was leading us in prayer (which he did in all the committee meetings), he asked God to show us if we were doing anything wrong to stop the flow of His blessings. God responded with a word like this: "You are on the right track. I am with you! Take courage and keep on going!"*

*These last few years remind me of the apostle Paul's words written in II Corinthians 4:8,9: "We are troubled on every side, yet not distressed; we are perplexed, but not in despair; persecuted, but not forsaken; cast down, <u>but not destroyed</u>!"*

*Although the daily struggle still remains, there is hope, and we have a leader filled with joy who is on the right track. AND GOD IS WITH HIM!*

Jeanne Alcott
Vice President for Partner Communications
Oral Roberts Evangelistic Association

## RICHARD ROBERTS — FULL OF THE SPIRIT OF JOY!

*Having been with Richard when he first encountered the spirit of joy gives me an unusual perspective on his experience. We were in Lakeland, Florida, at Carpenter's Home Church, and Richard was just taking over the service when laughter began breaking out sporadically in various sections of the congregation. Richard had been told about this phenomenon, but he had had no personal experience along those lines, so at first he seemed unsure of how to deal with it.*

*That night in the evening service, the laughter continued until Richard started to sing a song. But he had barely begun singing when the joy of the Lord hit him too! Strangely enough, he just stopped singing in the middle of his song and started laughing,* *almost violently, and yet hilariously, in the Spirit! This was unlike Richard, as his professional singing background had always demanded that he finish a number <u>no matter what</u>. This continued throughout the service as he tried his best to finish his sermon, but he simply couldn't keep from entering into the experience of the joy.*

*I didn't doubt the genuineness of the experience, but since I hadn't received it personally, I could only manage a couple of snickers and chuckles during that particular service.* ***Of course, watching Richard Roberts seemingly make a fool of himself was quite a delight!*** *My first thought was, "I hope this helps him, because the strain of ORU's debt has been overwhelming to him and to all of us."*

*As we traveled home together the next day, I wondered if the experience would last or if it was just a one-time thing. My question was soon answered as Richard broke out into hysterical laughter for no reason whatsoever in the crowded cabin of that airliner.* ***Was he ever getting some strange looks!*** *I tried to appear sane so that any of those watching who thought we were together would at least realize that he had someone to look after him!*

*When we returned to the reality of a debt of $42 million, it was a very sobering experience. We were facing monumental problems trying to keep the university operating, with our expenses far exceeding our cash available. I often wondered what people would have thought if they had known how little cash we had. Here we were, operating a $50-million enterprise with less cash in our bank accounts than many individuals have!*

*We would meet each day to look at the cash avail-*

able from that day's deposits and also the pressing expenses, many of which were already overdue. It seemed as if there was never enough cash in our hands to meet the needs of the day.

Usually, after we had conducted as much business as possible, those meetings turned into prayer meetings <u>because we were so overwhelmed by the problems</u>. Many times God would minister to us right there in the meeting, either through a word of knowledge, a prophecy, or simply a quiet reassurance that He would take care of us.

Quite often we were at the point of knowing we would not make it through the day without a miracle. An answer was always provided. Sometimes it was a new idea we hadn't thought of before. Often it was a supernatural act of God to give us favor with a vendor or creditor. Many times it was an unexpected source of revenue through a donation, a will bequest, or other avenue.

Truly this was a test of faith, with God teaching us that He would provide. **But it seemed He would only provide our daily bread!** We never had enough money to set aside for the future. Throughout this time, we began to realize what an incredible walk of faith this ministry is and the price that has been paid over the years by the founder, Oral Roberts, and so many others who have helped him along the way.

After Richard experienced the joy of the Lord, his countenance changed. Instead of being driven to try to "make things happen" to "save the ship," he began to laugh at our problems! Of course, there were times when we thought he might have gone a little bit over the edge, knowing the overwhelming responsibility he felt and the hopeless-

*looking situation we were facing,*

Our concerns grew at times when we felt he wasn't taking our situation seriously enough — especially when the daily problems happened to be centered on our own areas of responsibility! But as he laughed at the obstacles, we would finally end up praising the Lord with him and leaving those problems in God's hands. It wasn't that we weren't concerned or that we weren't working our dead-level best to solve the issues. It was a knowing that we were in God's will and that somehow, some way, He would make a way.

After Richard received the joy of the Lord, some of the rest of us had the opportunity to experience a fresh touch of joy for ourselves, too, as the joy broke out in our campus revivals and other services. Gradually, we gained a greater understanding of what God was doing in Richard and what He was doing in us.

We are still in a critical situation, fighting for our existence. It is still a daily walk of faith requiring our full dependence upon God, but we have an assurance in our hearts that God is with us. We will be able to handle the stress. We will face our mountains and make it over the top. There *is* a future for Oral Roberts University and our ministry, and there *is* a future for us personally.

God is answering our prayers as we allow the joy of the Lord to work through us to lift us and each other UP! Richard is full — and we are all full — of Holy Ghost joy!

George Fisher
Vice President for University Relations
Oral Roberts University

## JESUS IS THE REASON
## FOR OUR JOY!

*When Richard Roberts first established the management team at Oral Roberts University, there were many days when our main objective was simply to pray and seek God's face on a multitude of financial issues for which we lacked the answers.*

*During the first six months that we met, we often found ourselves struggling to answer the financial challenges in our own human strength. That is not to say that we were any less spiritual then than now; it was just that our main focus at that time was on our desperate financial needs.*

*As the first step toward getting out of debt and moving into financial freedom, Richard announced that we would go back to a previous commitment of giving 10 percent of our total ministry income to missions, ministries, and other needs as they were brought to our attention. We were going to start tithing again.*

*Then Richard was invited to preach at Carpenter's Home Church in Lakeland, Florida. When he returned, he was fired up to implement a brand-new direction, not only for the ministry and the university but also for the management team. His proclamation to each of us was that he had been touched by the "joy of the Lord" and he had also discovered that he could have joy in the midst of all the financial challenges and difficulties which we were facing.*

*That was when Richard officially instituted the "commandment" of his new position as President and Chief Executive Officer of ORU: to refuse to let the financial burdens steal the joy of our salvation.*

*This definitely sounded like something that each of us on the management team could certainly get fired up about, **IF** we only had the money we needed. Not only did we lack the money to pay the pressing needs of insurance, taxes, and payroll, but we were also facing a $42-million indebtedness!*

*I recall one particular morning when we added up our immediate needs and found that they totaled in excess of $900,000. Then we discovered that our cash reserves for that day were zero. The meeting was very quiet that morning. When the money runs out, you simply get quiet.*

*At Richard's direction, we asked Jeanne Alcott to pray. During her prayer, she prophesied that we would one day laugh at our current position and the fact that we had no money. She also said that we would rejoice because we had seen the way God had met every financial need.*

*By this time, Richard was laughing hysterically. I'm not sure if he was caught up in the joy of the Lord or if what she was saying struck him as funny because it seemed so impossible!*

*Later that same day, God provided a check for $1 million — more than enough to meet those needs! What an impressive display that was to each of us of God's ability to answer our prayers!*

*As the months passed, our needs always seemed to be met, many times only after we had reached the point of desperation. Each time we ran out of human possibilities, the Lord would provide.*

*I remember one morning when my heart was particularly heavy with a concern for our finances and the continuation of the ministry. I knew that in my state* *of mind Richard was bound to call on me to pray that morning. And he did! <u>That was one of the days when our prayers ended in laughter!</u>*

*Surely our joy is not because we are out of debt, but rather because we are <u>getting</u> out of debt. Our total indebtedness has been reduced from $42 million to about $21.5 million. I suspect that as time goes on, debt reduction will become less and less of an objective. Then we'll be able to focus more on the continuing goal of educating young men and women to spread the gospel message throughout the world.*

*Due to the pressures of overwhelming financial responsibilities, we've occasionally been distracted from that objective. But this has been our founding purpose <u>and will continue to be our purpose until the Lord returns</u>! Day by day, we are each trying to remember that Jesus Christ is not only the salvation for our soul, <u>**but He is the real reason for our joy!**</u>*

Gary Gibson
Director of Security
Oral Roberts University

## I CHOOSE THE JOY!

*As a child growing up in the church, one of the earliest gospel choruses I remember is, "The Joy of the Lord Is My Strength." At that time I did not know that the chorus comes from Nehemiah 8:10, "The joy of the Lord is your strength."*

*However, the full meaning of the "joy of the Lord" did not come alive in my heart until I saw it revolutionize the spiritual leadership of the Presi-*

dent of *Oral Roberts University, Richard Roberts, in late August of 1993. At that time Richard had been the second President and Chief Executive Officer of ORU for just seven months. They had been difficult months because along with the "joys" of being president, Richard was also saddled with the "joys" of being the chief executive officer of an institution that was $42 million in debt.*

*During those first seven months, joy had been a pretty scarce commodity as President Roberts and the management team met on a daily basis to decide how our scarce resources were going to be distributed among the desperate needs of the university. The cash almost always ran out before the bills were paid or before the payroll was met.*

*I have had the experience in my own life of returning thanks for a meal without having any idea under the sun where the next meal was coming from. The management team met at nine o'clock each morning to pray the prayer, "Give us this day our daily bread." The miracle is that God answered that prayer — in miraculous ways — day after day. But we were much more aware of the need, of the struggle, and of the burden, than we were of the joy of the Lord.*

*In late August of 1993, President Roberts went to Lakeland, Florida, to speak in Carpenter's Home Church, the church pastored by the Reverend Karl Strader, a member of the Oral Roberts University Board of Regents. Evangelist Rodney Howard-Browne from South Africa had just completed an extended series of evangelistic crusade services in the church. During those services, the joy of the Lord fell on the people and completely revolutionized the church.*

*When President Roberts preached there, the joy of*

*the Lord fell on him and completely transformed his life and ministry! This miraculous event is chronicled in the* Joy, Joy, Joy! *video prepared for the Partners of the Oral Roberts and Richard Roberts Ministries. If you have not seen that video, I highly recommend it to you. Many have told us that the joy of the Lord came into their lives as they were watching the video of President Roberts' experience.*

*After President Roberts returned to Tulsa from Carpenter's Home Church, the financial challenges facing the university were the same, but a "different" man was leading the management team in dealing with them. As President Roberts shared with us his personal experience, the joy of the Lord came into our lives and transformed us. On a number of occasions, in the midst of facing cash shortages of $50,000, $100,000, or more on a given day, President Roberts would burst into uncontrollable laughter — and the joy of the Lord would transform him and us as we faced those situations. The problems were not any less, but the God we served in His joy was so much greater than the problems we faced!*

*On one occasion when we were faced with what seemed like insurmountable needs, instead of the doubt, fear, and struggle that we had known before, the joy of the Lord was strong in our hearts. We knew that He who is in us is stronger than he who is in the world (see I John 4:4). From an entirely unexpected source, an alumnus of ORU drove to Tulsa and put a check for $1 million — that cashed — into the hands of President Roberts. We knew God was sovereignly in control of Oral Roberts University! We had an old-fashioned "Jericho march" around the table in the conference room to celebrate that victory! Where the* *joy of the Lord is, there is peace, rest, hope, and the supply of our needs.*

*On another occasion when we were faced with financial needs that could have put the university in jeopardy and there was no human way to meet them, instead of doom and gloom, President Roberts led us in a time of praise and worship from the joy that filled his heart. When we had peace as a group and felt the joy of the Lord strong in our hearts, President Roberts said, "This is a good day to die."*

*What he meant by that was that we had done everything we knew to do to obey God at ORU. We had made personnel changes to put our house in order. We had examined our priorities and motives. We were right in the center of God's will. We had done all we knew to do to stand, and now we were in God's hands — "This is a good day to die."*

*The joy of the Lord was strong in our hearts. We had prayed and praised together. There had been strong words of encouraging prophecy. We were strong in the Lord. You already know that we did not die. The pressing needs with which we were struggling were met. The joy of the Lord was our strength then and continues to be now.*

*In the intervening months, President Roberts' ministry and his leadership as the Chief Executive Officer of ORU have moved to a higher level. The joy of the Lord has become part of his ministry across America. Churches and hearts are being transformed. This joy has also made a tremendous impact on the spiritual life of Oral Roberts University. Spontaneous laughter in the Holy Spirit is not unusual in our chapel services and in our worship. Revival services conducted by Evangelist Rodney Howard-Browne have deepened and strengthened the experience of joy on the campus.*

*The joy of the Lord and an entirely different way of facing challenges and dealing with them have been evident in President Roberts' life. I have been a member of the management team without the clear manifestation of the joy of the Lord in our hearts, and I've also been a member with that joy clearly in evidence. **I choose the joy!***

*The joy of the Lord has transformed our lives and brought joy to our prayers of, "Give us this day our daily bread." And praise the Lord, He is doing just that!*

Dr. Carl H. Hamilton, Provost
Oral Roberts University

## NOW WE'RE LIVING
## IN THE MIDST OF A MIRACLE!

*At the time Richard Roberts was elected President and Chief Executive Officer of Oral Roberts University, he began what I believed was to be the final phase of his preparation for the leadership of the university. From January to June of 1993, Richard began to understand in a greater way the enormity of the task at hand, and he knew that it would require a strong spiritual leader who would not compromise God's Word and His promises for ORU — **someone who would make certain that the university never leaves its founding purpose.***

*I believe Richard is that strong spiritual leader, the one called of God to lead Oral Roberts University. When he took over the reins of ORU and began to dredge through the daily paperwork, suddenly the heartaches of the day-to-day operations — all the financial figures, the due dates for a multitude of bills — were staring him in the face. As Richard often says in his sermons, "It's one thing to have your lunch on the table, but it's another thing to have it in your stomach." Suddenly ORU "got into his stomach" — into his "belly."*

*Like a woman who becomes pregnant, Richard began the painstaking task of giving birth to his leadership role as President and Chief Executive Officer of ORU. He labored long and hard and met with the management team each day, striving to accomplish the task before him. With the direction of God and the spiritual knowledge that ORU was his "baby," he made it through that painful time of transition. He believed God and never compromised. He drew a line in the sand and refused to move it. Only Richard could have drawn that line, AND THE BUCK STOPPED WITH HIM.*

*It's the same way when a pregnant woman goes into labor. She can have all the encouragement, all the coaching, and all the medical help possible, BUT THE BUCK STOPS WITH HER. She is the one who is carrying the baby, and it is up to her to go through the pain of bringing it into the world. But when that baby is born, there's a special bond a mother has with her baby which no one else in the world can have with that child!*

*Richard's dad, Chancellor Oral Roberts, has that kind of bond with ORU. And now that same kind of bond exists between Richard and ORU. The bond may be even greater for Richard than it is for Chancellor Roberts because not only has our heavenly Father* called and equipped Richard to lead ORU, but his earthly father recognizes that God has called and equipped him — <u>and in that Chancellor Roberts has told me he is pleased beyond words!</u> **At age seventy-seven he can rest in the knowledge that ORU's future is secure.**

I do not believe that Richard could have withstood the pressures of the past two years if he had not been called of God to be the President of ORU. Just as the pregnant woman is the only one who can carry the baby and nurture it during pregnancy and then bring it to birth, it took someone who was called of God to nurture ORU's miracle and then bring it to birth.

Richard has surrounded himself with the needed support staff to assist him, just as a woman in labor surrounds herself with a team of doctors and nurses to help her. She is the focal point, but she knows they are there to help her . . . AND THEY ARE ALL BELIEVING FOR THE SAME POSITIVE RESULTS!

In the midst of all the painful events he was going through at ORU, Richard found the joy of the Lord, <u>and it sustained him.</u> **And the joy was ample enough to sustain those around him too!** It's as if God knew the pain of "delivering" ORU's miracle would be too great, so He gave Richard the joy as a "spiritual epidural," so to speak, just as a doctor would give an epidural to a pregnant woman to numb her to the pain of delivery. The joy of the Lord had the dulling effect of an epidural so he could withstand the warfare and still enjoy and experience the birth. Without that spiritual epidural, Richard might have been destroyed by the pain of giving birth to ORU's miracle.

It is said that during the early years of the United States space program, we didn't need a miracle to go to the moon. However, when some of our space missions encountered serious difficulties, <u>we needed a miracle to bring our men home safely</u>. When Chancellor Oral Roberts founded Oral Roberts University, he needed a miracle to establish this university. But, later, when Richard took over the "mission," <u>we had to have a miracle to continue this great work for God</u>. **AND NOW WE'RE LIVING IN THE MIDST OF THAT MIRACLE!**

> Harry Salem II
> Executive Director of TV Productions
> Oral Roberts Evangelistic Association

## WITH THE WATER
## YOU GET THE WET!

This group of faithful men and women who have shared their testimonies, as well as others who are a part of my team, have seen me at my best and they've seen me at my worst. They've seen me exactly as I am, in all of my humanness. They've seen me grappling with troubles which have torn my insides out. They've seen me standing strong with my faith, *AND THEY'VE STOOD WITH ME ALL THE WAY — EVEN WHEN WE WERE STANDING ON THE EDGE OF THE PRECIPICE!*

Above all, they've heard my battle cry when the devil has reached out to take a deadly swipe at us. What is my battle cry? *"Seek ye first the kingdom of God, and his righteousness; AND ALL THESE THINGS SHALL BE ADDED UNTO YOU"* (Matthew 6:33).

Why on earth would I pick that verse for my battle cry? The Lord revealed to me that in my burning desire to see ORU break free from debt, I had begun to focus too much on the *things* that we needed — the business deals, the sale of properties which I had hoped would catapult us out of debt.

God really drove this home to me through a soul-searching message which our dear friend, the Reverend Kenneth Hagin, Jr., preached on this passage from Matthew, chapter 6. His words sank deep into my spirit that day, and I felt as if the Lord was telling me, "Richard, stop seeking My hand. Just seek My face, and you'll get My hand too!" ***WITH THE WATER YOU GET THE WET!***

At the close of the service, Brother Ken's words leaped out at me as he began to relate this sobering story: "There were times when we were constructing this building (the beautiful Rhema Bible Church sanctuary) when there was absolutely no more money. The devil was mocking me, saying, 'It took your father all of these years to build Rhema Bible Training Center, and now you're going to destroy it in less than two years.'"

Then Brother Ken exclaimed, "I had to fight those words off in the spirit <u>and seek God first</u>! I even took my Bible over to the window and set it down on the floor, and I actually stood on my Bible while I looked out at that construction site!"

Now that was a soul-shaking word to me, my friend! *And it hit me right on my bull's-eye!* Brother Ken may have been preaching to many people in that crowded auditorium, but that word was aimed directly at me. <u>You see, I was walking down that same lonely road</u>!

Then he began to prophesy by the Spirit, saying, "The Lord has seen you. You have walked upright before Him, you have persevered, **and now God is going to answer."** Oh, glory be to the Lord, I took that as a powerful word from God for me, *and that Scripture from Matthew 6:33 has become the battle cry for my life!*

After that service was over, the Lord reminded me that when Moses stood on the shore of the Red Sea, he didn't cry out to God about the mighty chariots of Pharaoh thundering up behind him. He didn't rant and rave to the Lord about all the rough, jagged rocks thrusting out of the water on the left and on the right, or the waves of the sea pounding against the shore.

Moses simply lifted his rod in the air and boldly proclaimed BY FAITH, "Fear ye not, stand still, and see the salvation of the Lord . . . for the Egyptians whom ye have seen to day, ye shall see them again no more for ever" (Exodus 14:13). **Moses lifted up a standard of faith before God!**

Now the people were moaning and groaning and grumbling, <u>but not Moses</u>. And as the leader of Oral Roberts University, *I must lift up a mighty standard of faith and declare, "We're going to seek the Lord FIRST! We're going to seek His face, His kingdom, and His righteousness!"*

I believe the whole secret of life is wrapped up in those powerful verses from Matthew, chapter 6. *God is saying to His people, "IF YOU'LL SEEK ME FIRST, MY KINGDOM, MY RIGHTEOUSNESS, ALL THE RICHES OF HEAVEN WILL BEGIN RAINING DOWN ON YOUR LIFE!"*

## Chapter 6

# THE JOY OF THE LORD IS YOUR STRENGTH!

When the joy of the Lord came into my life, it was like a great torrent of Holy Ghost power came flooding up in me, surging from the very depths of my soul! All of a sudden, a mighty, sovereign move of the Spirit swept over my whole being like a powerful rushing wind from Heaven.

This Holy Ghost joy and laughter hit my life in much the same way that it must have hit the disciples of Jesus on the Day of Pentecost. Acts 2:1-4 declares that they were gathered in the Upper Room, when SUDDENLY they were engulfed by the sound of a mighty rushing wind from Heaven, and the Spirit of God descended upon them in the form of cloven tongues of fire. They were all filled with the Holy Ghost and began to speak with other tongues as the Spirit of God gave them utterance.

Now I want you to listen with your whole heart to what the Bible says happened next. Devout men of every nation were dwelling in Jerusalem at that time, and when the power of God burst forth like a tidal wave from the Upper Room, **the multitudes were confounded** be-**cause they heard those men speaking in their own languages!**

I mean, there were Parthians, Medes, Elamites, those from Mesopotamia, from Judaea, from Cappadocia, from Pontus — in other words, from all the regions of the known world of that day. Those foreigners were gathered in Jerusalem for the great harvest festival, when suddenly they heard the disciples of Jesus, the men from Galilee, speaking in the dialects of the foreigners' native lands.

Then Peter, who was no doubt bubbling over with the Holy Ghost, stood to his feet and proclaimed, "These are not drunken, as ye suppose, since it is but the third hour of the day [nine o'clock in the morning]. But this is that which was spoken by the prophet Joel; and it shall come to pass in the last days, saith God, I will pour out my Spirit upon all flesh: and your sons and your daughters shall prophesy, and your young men shall see visions, and your old men shall dream dreams" (Acts 2:15-17).

When those men of faith burst forth from the Upper Room on the Day of Pentecost, **the whole world thought they were drunk!** Peter had to announce to the multitude which had gathered, "These men haven't been drinking alcohol! After all, it's only nine o'clock in the morning, and the Jerusalem bars aren't open yet! NO, THEY'RE DRUNK ON THE NEW WINE OF THE SPIRIT!"

I tell you, there's a fresh new move of the Spirit afoot across America today, and God is once again restoring His holy joy and laughter to the church! We're beginning to draw water from the wells of salvation, AND WE'RE DOING IT WITH GREAT JOY! (See Isaiah 12:3.)

> **Oh, that every born-again believer would receive a fresh baptism of the joy of the Lord *and that it would come upon them SUDDENLY like it came into my life and the lives of those disciples in Jerusalem!***

Why do I believe so strongly that we must have a fresh baptism of Holy Ghost joy? Because much of the body of Christ today is beaten down. They're beaten down in their spirits. They're beaten down in their churches. They feel disheartened and downtrodden because of church splits, because of brutal assaults from the secular news media. They feel browbeaten by the troubles and heartaches of life. Their heads are down. They feel subservient to the world.

Really, it seems as if the devil has trampled them in the dust. They've been whipped by satan and all of his demons, and they're just waiting for his next deadly missile to come ripping through their lives. Many don't have a strong witness for the Lord because they have no joy. **And I know exactly how they feel because when this Holy Ghost laughter exploded in my life, I was a man who had no joy!**

I had sunk so low that I'd almost forgotten the Scripture in Nehemiah 8:10, which says, "The joy of the Lord is your strength." No wonder I felt like I was at the bottom of the barrel! I had no joy, <u>so I had no strength</u>! The Bible also declares in Ephesians 6:10, "Be strong in the Lord — be empowered through your union with Him; draw your strength from Him — that strength which His [boundless] might provides" (AM-PLIFIED). All of a sudden it dawned on me that there was just no way I could be strong in the Lord <u>unless I was full of the joy of the Lord WHICH IS MY STRENGTH</u>!

Can you imagine a heavyweight boxing champion going into the ring for a championship fight *after spending two weeks lying flat on his back in a hospital room?* I mean, he's had IVs hooked up to his body, and they've been drawing blood every day and running every imaginable test on him.

Finally, AFTER TWO WEEKS IN THE HOSPITAL, they release him only hours before he is scheduled to take on one of his leading contenders in a world championship title bout. What on earth would he do? Well, I imagine any fighter in that position would postpone the fight *<u>until his strength could be renewed!</u>*

Many Christians today are staggering out onto the battlefield of life, desperately trying to rally for one last stand for Christ! **But they'll never be able to stand tall for Jesus without the joy of the Lord <u>which is their strength</u>!**

What does the Bible say? Isaiah 40:31 declares, "They that wait upon the Lord shall renew their strength; they shall mount up with wings as eagles; they shall run and not be weary; and they shall walk, and not faint." But the key to those remarkable verses lies in WAITING UPON THE LORD. As you wait upon the Lord, as you linger in His presence, you're going to find yourself overflowing with the joy of the Lord, *because in His presence there is FULL-NESS of joy!* (See Psalm 16:11.)

That's what this fresh baptism of joy is all about!

The Lord Himself said in John 15:11 that He wants our joy to be FULL! Not just a weak little halfhearted trickle of joy bubbling up in our souls every now and then. Not just a tiny splashing stream of Holy Ghost joy and laughter flowing through our lives occasionally. But a mighty rushing RIVER of the joy of the Lord pouring through our being every day of our lives! *THAT'S WHAT THE LORD DESIRES FOR US!*

Now I want you to turn in your Bible to Proverbs 17:22, which says, "A happy heart is a good medicine and a cheerful mind works healing" (AMPLIFIED). There are some doctors today who will tell you, "If I can get a patient's spirit up, he or she has a much better chance of fully recovering." And there are some hospitals in this country where they'll actually invite a comedian into the patients' rooms just to try to make them laugh. Why? Because even the secular world understands that laughter boosts your spirit! Even the medical profession has grasped that a merry heart, a heart full of joy and laughter, *WORKS LIKE A POWERFUL MEDICINE!*

The rest of that verse in Proverbs 17:22 declares, "A broken spirit dries the bones." Have you ever met someone who is as dry and brittle as a bone? I mean, they're so negative that when they walk into a room, it feels like somebody got up and walked out! *I'll tell you what — someone like that is a candidate for a fresh baptism of the joy of the Lord!*

Now turn back a few pages in your Bible to Proverbs 15:15: "All the days of the desponding afflicted are made evil [by anxious thoughts and foreboding], but he who has a glad heart has a continual feast [**regardless of circumstances**]" (AMPLIFIED).

I want you to notice that this Scripture does not

deny the fact that negative circumstances exist. There are some people in the world today who try to deny the reality of negative circumstances, insisting that that's real faith. **No, that's denial.** I never deny that satan is my adversary or that he's roaming this earth as a roaring lion, seeking whom he may devour. I just let that mighty river of joy come FLOODING up in my soul, *which gives me the strength to stand against the devil and command him to flee!*

## I HAD NO EARTHLY IDEA HOW TO COUNT IT ALL JOY!

The apostle James added another dimension to this subject of Holy Ghost joy when he wrote in James 1:2-4: "Consider it wholly joyful, my brethren, whenever you are enveloped in or encounter trials of any sort, or fall into various temptations. Be assured and understand that the trial and proving of your faith brings out endurance and steadfastness and patience. But let endurance and steadfastness and patience have full play and do a thorough work, so that you may be [people] perfectly and fully developed (with no defects), lacking in nothing" (AMPLIFIED).

I had no earthly idea how to count it all joy when I was engulfed by that mind-boggling avalanche of bills and debt! I guess you could say that I hadn't really locked in on that Scripture in James, chapter 1.

Oh, I had grasped what the apostle James meant when he talked about being enveloped in various trials and tribulations. I KNEW I WAS FACING THE FIERCEST OPPOSITION OF MY LIFE, **but I couldn't imagine how to count it all joy!**

What a difference it made when that fresh baptism of Holy Ghost joy and laughter swept over my life! I could feel the joy bubbling up in my soul, even when it looked as though I was hurtling over the edge of a cliff!

Almost the instant I arrived back in Tulsa after that fateful trip to Lakeland, Florida, the devil decided to throw a test at me. Isn't it amazing how, when something good happens, satan always seems to show up on your doorstep, sneering at you, "We'll see if this thing is real or not!"

The test cropped up in the middle of one of our financial meetings when the telephone rang, and one of my associates answered it. "We need $85,000 to pay for the university's insurance, *and we've got to have it by two o'clock this afternoon,*" he said. Now, in the natural, I knew what this meant. We had not been able to pay this particular bill for some time. The company had given us a final deadline. Unless we paid it, our entire insurance would be cancelled. However, when I received this word, I burst into a fit of Holy Ghost laughter! And the man who had answered the phone was absolutely <u>certain</u> that I had lost it!

Now let me remind you, I am a person who is usually in control. I simply do not break down laughing at problems of that magnitude — especially when they're due by two o'clock the same afternoon! But in the next split second, I was laughing so hard that I slid out of my chair and landed in a heap in the middle of the floor! And that's where I was glued <u>for at least ten more minutes</u>, laughing uncontrollably with the joy of the Lord!

As God is my witness, it was no more than twenty minutes later when the telephone rang, and the same man answered the phone. All of a sudden, his face turned as white as a sheet. "Richard," he blurted out, "you're not going to believe this, but we just got a check in the mail for $243,000!" *And I fell out of my chair again, laughing hysterically in the Spirit!*

Suddenly, everyone in the room was laughing with me! I mean, you could just feel the gut-wrenching pressure being released! All at once my associates <u>knew</u> that the joy was real, and we had a hallelujah Jericho victory march around the conference table!

Friend, before I received that fresh baptism of joy, there's no way I could have mustered up even a weak smile or a halfhearted chuckle when my associate gave me that shattering piece of news. <u>I would have been the one turning as white as a sheet</u>! But God has filled me with HIS supernatural power to laugh even when satan is shooting his biggest guns at me! *I'm learning how to count it all joy <u>even when it looks like the devil has the upper hand</u>!*

## I HAVE EVIDENCE THAT THE JOY OF THE LORD WORKS!

My mind flashes back to another moment when we were all gathered around that same conference table, facing a monstrous pile of bills, and with absolutely no money to pay them. But as we began to pray, instead of an atmosphere of gloom and doom, there was a buoyancy in our spirits and an unshakable expectancy for miracles! Out of the blue, a man walked into my office and declared, "God has told me to give you a million dollars!" Oh, glory be to the Lord!

Now I had never breathed a word about those staggering needs to anyone. But when that man handed me his million-dollar check, I felt so high in the Lord that I literally fell off my couch, laughing hilariously in the Spirit! I was absolutely speechless! Why? Because I was filled to overflowing with joy <u>unspeakable</u> and full of glory!

It was only a month or two later when that same man showed up at my office again with some more wonderful news: "God has told me to give you another million dollars!" And several months after that he called me again, saying, "God has told me to give you another million dollars." Every time I was greeted with some more thrilling news, I found myself laughing spontaneously, uncontrollably — *filled with a spirit of Holy Ghost joy!*

Now I praise and thank God for that man's obedient spirit, BUT IF I HADN'T RECEIVED THE JOY OF THE LORD, I don't believe I could have stayed under the victory cloud of God! I mean, if I had been frantic, just beside myself with fear, God's heavenly supply line might have been cut off! But when God poured out the joy of the Lord in my heart, *He flung His heavenly supply line WIDE OPEN!*

> **While I was counting it all joy, taking my Holy Ghost-joy medicine every day, one by one God was sweeping those forbidding mountains right out of my path!**

It wasn't long until I received a call from a man representing a company in Oklahoma City. He said that his company wanted to forgive a $500,000 debt against ORU. He told me, "Mr. Roberts, God has spoken to my heart, and I want to change the $500,000 debt to an outright contribution to Oral Roberts University." I was absolutely speechless. I was just laughing too hard.

During that same time period, the owner of a company in Florida, to whom ORU owed $60,000, heard that I was scheduled to preach in that state. He contacted me, saying, "Richard, I would like to meet with you." Now I knew we didn't have the $60,000 we owed him, but somehow I managed to scrape together $10,000 to give him as a gesture of good faith, hoping he would continue to carry the balance.

After I presented that man with our check, he said, "Richard, my wife and I have a great love for ORU, and we want our children to attend college there. We've prayed about this and would like to make the rest of ORU's $60,000 debt a direct contribution to the university." Well, I just began laughing *with the joy of the Lord! And that's exactly what God had said would happen while I watched Him pay off our debt!*

Not long after that, there was another company to whom the university owed $470,000. By the grace of God, we were able to negotiate an arrangement with them to pay $55,000 in cash, along with loaning them some historic videos which our ministry owned, and they wiped out the entire debt!

> *Friend, I tell you, I'm on to something here!* In one fell swoop we had over $1 million of out-and-out debt forgiveness!

89

I'll never forget the time I was facing a certain business deal concerning a "depressed" piece of property which the university owned. Have you ever been depressed over a depressed piece of property? You see, it had been appraised at $3.3 million, and one particular group had offered me the appraised value, but I turned them down flat *because I believed God had given me a specific price for that property — $5 million!*

When the bankers heard what had happened, they went ballistic! They told me in no uncertain terms, "You should sell that property at the appraised value. It's a good price." *But I said no.*

A few weeks later, the same group came back to me and said, "We're now prepared to offer you $3.8 million." But I still refused to sell. Well, this time the bankers were *outraged,* and they chewed me out royally! They informed me, "You won't get one penny more for that piece of property!" And when I left their office, I felt as if I needed to bandage myself up because of the verbal whipping I had taken!

By this time, quite a few people were beginning to think I was crazy, and I was starting to ask the Lord myself, "God, are You sure about this?" But I held on to the amount that I believed He had given me, and pretty soon I received an offer of $5 million — **the exact amount the Lord had spoken in my heart!**

**You see, I have evidence that the joy of the Lord works! <u>I've got living proof that God's holy joy and laughter can break you free from satan's snare</u>!** Before I received this happy, hilarious joy, I was getting beaten up in just about every area of my life, desperately wishing I could step over into God's stream of blessing! *BUT NOW, I'VE BROKEN*

## *LOOSE FROM THAT HELLISH BONDAGE, AND I'M MARCHING ON TO VICTORY IN THE PROMISED LAND!*

### THE WHOLE CAMPUS WAS VIBRATING WITH A FRESH SPIRIT OF JOY!

After that mighty revival of joy hit the ORU campus in 1993, our Board of Regents met for its regular fall meeting. Really, the whole campus was vibrating with a fresh spirit of joy and holy laughter! One evening several of our board members were the guests of Lindsay and me on Trinity Broadcasting Network's *Praise the Lord* program. Here's what they had to say about this extraordinary new baptism of Holy Ghost joy!

First of all, Karl Strader, pastor of Carpenter's Home Church in Lakeland, Florida, shared this testimony of the incredible outpouring of joy which had exploded in his church:

*There were about five hundred churches that just "crashed our party" with the Holy Ghost. The power of God fell all over the place, and people were filled with holy laughter. Between seven thousand and eight thousand people gave their hearts to the Lord in our church alone. People who were carrying heavy burdens found their burdens being lifted. Why? Because the kingdom of God is not meat and drink; it's righteousness and peace and **JOY** in the Holy Ghost! (See Romans 14:17.)*

*A couple of our elders who were in the revival meetings left to go on a world preaching tour, and the first country they visited was Russia. Now if anybody has any reason to be depressed and downtrodden, it's* the Russians, because even though communism has lifted, <u>they don't know what's going to happen tomorrow</u>. Most Russian people just don't laugh. They have nothing to laugh about! **But in those meetings, 99 percent of the people were on the floor, stacked like cordwood, laughing hysterically!**

Then those same elders went to Manila, where their children are missionaries. One told his father, "Dad, these people will not laugh. Orientals don't respond that way." Well, everybody in the church fell to the floor under the power. <u>They were laughing all over the place</u>! And the same thing happened in Singapore. Then the elders went to Uganda, Kenya, and several other African countries, and wherever they went, the same thing happened!

I believe this revival is the beginning of something that's going to sweep around the world! **<u>As the forces of evil are increasing everywhere, God is lifting up a standard, and we're going to see a mighty tidal wave of revival upon this earth!</u>**

Next, I want you to read what Marilyn Hickey, chairman of the Board of Regents of ORU, had to say about the way this amazing Holy Ghost revival of joy has affected her life. Marilyn and her husband, Wally, pastor Happy Church in Denver, Colorado:

Rodney Howard-Browne was in Denver for three weeks, and the first night I went, I saw people laughing, people falling [under the power], but I just sat there and cried. <u>I knew it was real</u>. I didn't understand what was going on, but I was so hungry for the manifested presence of God! I can't say that I was dry or depressed, but I was just hungry for God.

My daughter, Sarah, came into town, and I told her, "I'm going over to Calvary Temple Sunday night.

*If you want to go, it's fine; but it's a little wild for you."*
*You see, she's very conservative. But she still decided*
*to go. And when Rodney came past us and said,*
*"Receive the joy of the Lord!" she fell into my lap*
*laughing, and then I fell laughing into the lap of some*
*stranger beside me!*

*The next night when the service was over, we*
*started walking out the door. She took my hand, and*
*I fell to the floor laughing. She fell, too, and people*
*couldn't get out the door without walking over us. I*
*said, "I know about being the doorkeeper in the house*
*of the Lord, but I haven't been a doormat before!"*

*For me, this experience was like renewing my first*
*love. When you first meet Jesus, He's so precious to*
*you, and His presence is so real. Well, that's what this*
*was like. It was a refreshing. It was like going on*
*vacation. And when the meetings were over, I loved*
*people with a new love. I felt such compassion for*
*them! We think joy does only one thing — it makes you*
*laugh. But when God moves on us, HE DOES WHAT*
*WE NEED HIM TO DO!*

Next, Pastor Carlton Pearson from Higher Dimen-
sions Family Church in Tulsa, Oklahoma, poured out
his heart concerning the biblical basis for this fresh
outbreak of Holy Ghost joy:

*One time I asked God if He ever laughed. You hear*
*of Him crying, and the whole world is crying. We're*
*crying because our houses are burning down, floods*
*have devastated our farmlands, our economy has gone*
*wild, there's crime in the streets, and blood is running*
*on the sidewalks. While the world is crying and*
*weeping, God is reminding the saints of the hope we*
*have in Christ.*

*When I asked God, "When do You laugh?" I discov-*

ered that there are only three references in the whole Bible to God's laughing, and they're all in the book of Psalms. In each instance, <u>He is laughing at His enemies</u>. Every single time, He is making fun and folly of the devil's attempt to thwart His plan. God is saying that through this new move of the Spirit, there's hope for the future and for the church, **and the blessing of this nation will come through the church.**

Now some people may not relate at all to what we're talking about, but I tell you, the joy of the Lord is our strength! People need laughter. People need joy. The Bible also says, "Thou shalt rejoice in the Lord" (Isaiah 41:16). And one of the Hebrew renderings of the word rejoice here means to jump up and spin wildly. On the Day of Pentecost, they thought the disciples were drunk. There had to be some reason for them to think that, didn't there? ***I BELIEVE THIS NEW MOVE OF GOD IS SCRIPTURAL!***

Dr. John Hagee, pastor of Cornerstone Church in San Antonio, Texas, delivered a very powerful word on the joy of the Lord:

*Solomon wrote in the Proverbs that "a merry heart doeth good like a medicine" (Proverbs 17:22). Jesus is the Great Physician, and He knows the medicine the soul needs when it's weary in well doing. And I believe God is giving His Bride a merry heart for a very depressing time.*

*Forty years ago, no one would ever have believed that we would live in a nation of drive-by shootings, condoms in the schools, prayer and the Bible being taken out of the schools. Everything that we hold dear has been debased. The church has been under relentless attack. It is a warfare of immeasurable intensity, <u>and the only relief from that is the joy of the Lord!</u>*

*On the other hand, there is no such thing as absolute euphoria every day of your life. Calvary was not a euphoric experience. Gethsemane was not a euphoric experience. But after it was over, it produced joy unspeakable!*

*Life is not wonderful every day of the world. There's an enduring element here that the body of Christ must grasp. You have to punch it through and stay steady and let God help you get it into the end zone.* **And when you get it into the end zone, then you can have your victory dance!**

*Now the fruit of the laughter is so very critical. There is a cult in Japan called the "laughter cult," and they go to the temple, flagellate themselves with roses, and laugh hysterically. But the end result of the laughter is emptiness. It is one thing to laugh to become happy; it is another thing to laugh BECAUSE YOU ARE HAPPY. One is a psychic phenomenon; one is caused by the Holy Ghost.*

*We are experiencing something of the Holy Ghost because it glorifies the Father. It's bringing families together, it's giving divine relief, and it's giving us the strength to go on! For years, I have incorporated humor in my own ministry because it is one of the only things that will bring relief to people who are suffering.*

*One of the devil's trump cards is to tell you that if you come to Jesus, you can never have another happy day, you'll never do anything that's fun again, your happy life is over.* **But you don't know what happiness is until you find the Lord. HE IS THE SOURCE OF JOY ITSELF.**

*I want you to know that you can be happy in an unhappy world! Happiness is a matter of choice. You can be happy in political oppression. You can be happy when the government is taxing you immeasurably and taking your civil rights from you. You can be happy in the darkest storm of your life!* Why? **BECAUSE JESUS CHRIST IS THERE!**

Our dear friend, Billy Joe Daugherty, pastor of Victory Christian Center here in Tulsa, Oklahoma, opened his heart and shared a very penetrating word about the joy of the Lord:

*One of the things that has blessed me through the years has been the revelation that God never changes. It doesn't matter what the circumstances are, what your feelings are, His Word is going to come through. It never alters.*

*Our feelings of joy or feelings of sadness are triggered by thoughts. When people start thinking good things, the joy starts exploding in their lives. You can start thinking, "I am redeemed from the curse! I am delivered! All things are working together for good!" and joy starts getting all over you!*

*Another thing [about the joy] is that when you reach out to people who are hurting — when you "send portions unto them for whom nothing [has been] prepared" (Nehemiah 8:10) — THEN the joy of the Lord will be your strength.*

*The Bible also says that a merry heart does you good like a medicine. Some people need to take the "God-pill," and then a lot of things will begin to open up to them. John 7:38 declares that out of your belly shall flow rivers of living water. Joy flows out of the spirit, revelation flows out of it, and healing flows out of it. That's why Proverbs 4:23 says to guard your heart (your spirit) with all diligence.*

*Now there's another aspect of the joy as we explore*

*all of these areas. Jesus said that there is joy in Heaven over one sinner who repents (see Luke 15:10). <u>And this is the hour of the greatest harvest!</u> We understand that it's a time of the greatest darkness the earth has ever seen, but simultaneously it is a time of the greatest harvest. **AND THAT MEANS THERE'S GOING TO BE MORE JOY IN THIS HOUR!***

Before the *Praise the Lord* program was over, Pastor Strader added one final word concerning why we, as Christians, have an absolutely unshakable reason to rejoice.

He said, ***"If we have nothing else to laugh about, we ought to be rejoicing exceedingly, with great joy, <u>BECAUSE OUR NAMES ARE WRITTEN IN THE LAMB'S BOOK OF LIFE!"</u>***

Oh, praise God! As Christians, we, above all people on the face of this earth, have EVERY reason to rejoice with unspeakable joy!

## THERE'S NO HANGOVER WITH THE JOY OF THE LORD!

Pastor Hagee put his finger on a key issue when he pointed out why he incorporates humor into his own ministry. He declared, *"It is one of the only things that will bring relief to people who are suffering."* Not only does joy-filled, Holy Ghost laughter bring an indescribable release from your suffering, but the joy of the Lord has produced in my life what I would call a "Holy Ghost numbness." Now that may not sound very appealing to you, but let's explore this a little bit further.

You see, when holy joy and laughter begin to flood through your being, it's like taking a strong dose of medicine to help numb you to the problem. When some people are struck by a terrible tragedy, they may decide to get bombed out of their minds on liquor. Why? *Because they're trying to numb themselves to their problems.* They may drink themselves into a drunken stupor just to escape from their troubles. You can get a brutal hangover from that kind of numbness, **BUT THERE'S NO HANGOVER FROM THE JOY OF THE LORD!**

Friend, the joy of the Lord is so refreshing! I tell you, it sure beats a cold beer! You see, I've been drinking down at "Joel's place" lately — **the prophet Joel's place!** I've been drinking from those rivers of living water, the wells of salvation <u>**that never run dry**</u>! *I've been drinking deep from the fountain where God's joy is overflowing! Oh, there's nothing else in the world like it! THE JOY OF THE SAVIOR HAS OVERTAKEN MY LIFE!*

# Chapter 7

# WOULD YOU RATHER HAVE A LAUGHING REVIVAL OR A CRYING REVIVAL?

There has been some criticism from certain church leaders. Some are calling this move of God the "laughing revival." Well, I just want to ask one question: "Would you rather have a crying revival?" I mean, haven't we all cried enough tears, like the old country-and-western songs say: "I Get Tears in My Beer," or, "Baby, You Done Sorta Stepped on My Aorta"?

Aren't you tired of crying? Wouldn't you rather have the joy of the Lord in your heart than a bucketful of tears? Or would you rather be melancholy? *You know — face like a melon, head like a collie!*

Maybe we should stop calling our churches the "Happy Church" or the "Victorious Church." Perhaps we should start calling them something like the "Growling Church," or the "Grumbling Church," or the "First Church of the Weeping Willow"!

Now if you'd rather have a permanent frown on your face, I'm not knocking it. <u>But the frown wasn't working for me</u>! Neither was the ulcer nor the sleepless nights. I had to have something fresh. **I HAD TO HAVE A REVOLUTIONARY CHANGE IN MY LIFE!**

I was absolutely flabbergasted when a minister friend of mine turned me down flat after I invited him to one of Brother Rodney Howard-Browne's services. He informed me that he could not support me in this revival of joy, and he would not come. <u>I mean, he was dead set against it</u>!

Then he added, "I have a philosophical objection to the emphasis on laughter." And I thought to myself, *Well, would you rather have an emphasis on frowning?* But I simply replied, "The emphasis isn't on laughter. The emphasis is on revival. **The emphasis is on repentance and on changed lives.**"

When I tell people that the joy of the Lord saved my life, I mean exactly that! ***The laughter did not save my life.*** It was the joy of the Lord which lifted me out of the devil's quagmire, *and I had been sinking fast!*

Laughter is not the mainstream of this brand-new move of God's Spirit. Laughter is merely a by-product. It's an outward manifestation of what's happening down deep on the inside in your innermost being. **THE MAINSTREAM IS A CHANGED HEART.**

Even though I was jolted by my friend's reaction, I went on to relate to him a most unusual experience I'd had during the revival at ORU. You see, I'm not a person who weeps very easily. But when Brother Rodney laid hands on me during one of the services, I fell to the floor under the power of God, and the Holy Spirit came upon me so strongly that I began weeping and shaking and sobbing uncontrollably.

While I was lying on the floor, completely broken before the Lord, God gave me an astonishing vision in my spirit. In the sweep of a moment, I saw the debt at ORU completely wiped away! I saw our endowment soaring and the enrollment bursting at the seams! I saw the students in the years to come streaming to the four corners of the earth with the healing Gospel of Jesus! In the *flash of a second, I saw it all!*

Now I've talked about the day when ORU will be out of debt, and I've clung fiercely to my faith that we will reach that goal. But for the very first time, a picture flashed through my mind of what I had been saying with my mouth. IN A MOMENT'S TIME, I SAW IT ALL, AND IT LITERALLY TORE ME UP!

Then I heard the Lord whispering in my heart, "Now that you've seen what you've only spoken of before, <u>you can decree it into being, **and what you saw will happen!**</u>" I was so broken up by what I saw in my spirit that I couldn't stop weeping! *And I made a fresh vow to the Lord to see that ORU never departs from its founding purpose!*

During that same service, Brother Rodney laid hands on our eight-year-old daughter, Olivia, and she told us later, "The Lord said to me, 'When you grow up, you're going to preach.'" Friend, that's my own flesh and blood talking, and it touches a strong chord in my heart! *I'm talking about changed lives here! I'm talking about a Heaven-opening, hell-shaking, Holy Ghost MOVE OF GOD'S SPIRIT!*

After I told my minister friend about my experience, I exclaimed, "If you owed $42 million, you'd want the joy of the Lord in your life too!" And then I added offhandedly, "By the way, the debt has already dropped to $26 million." (And as I'm writing this book, it's plunged another $4.5 million to $21.5 million!) Well, he immediately wanted to know how that had happened, and I replied, "You ought to come to the service and find out!"

*Friend, there are some people who don't want to put*

*their big toe into God's SUDDENLY!* But I don't want to merely dip my big toe into the water. I want to dive down deep into the flow of God's Spirit. ***I WANT TO BE READY AT A MOMENT'S NOTICE TO MOVE WITH THE VICTORY CLOUD OF GOD!***

## DON'T THROW THE BABY OUT WITH THE BATHWATER!

There's another hurdle that some people have to get over before they can dive into the river of God's joy. You see, some have expressed the feeling that this Holy Ghost laughter seems to be fake. They believe that some people are getting over into the flesh with the joy of the Lord.

Friend, even if some are getting over into the flesh, that doesn't mean that you and I can get by without a full dose of the joy of the Lord! As a dear preacher friend of mine once put it, *"I'd rather have a little wildfire than no fire at all!"*

No doubt there are some who are getting over into the flesh with this brand-new move of the Spirit, **but we are flesh.** I believe it's far more dangerous to stifle the move of God simply because a few people are getting into the flesh. I'd rather deal with those few on an individual basis and help them see that they're in the flesh. There should be some admonition and teaching in this area, <u>along with the moving of the Spirit</u>. **BUT LET'S NOT THROW THE BABY OUT WITH THE BATHWATER!**

Really, I don't know of anyone who was any more skeptical of this joy-filled, Holy Ghost move of the Spirit than my wife, Lindsay. So I've asked her to describe to you exactly how God helped her resolve those feelings of skepticism:

*Richard's mother, Evelyn, tried to explain to me what was going on in this revival of joy because there was no way I could figure it out logically. You see, I have an analytical mind. I have to have a logical, rational explanation for everything. It's just my personality! And maybe you have an analytical mind, too, so I hope what I'm about to say will help you.*

*Before Richard went to Lakeland, I knew something was going to hit him, but I didn't have any earthly idea what IT was. I had absolutely no clue. I had grown up in a mainline denomination, so I'd had no experience with Pentecost during my early life. When I married Richard, that was my introduction to Pentecost. Growing up, if it wasn't in our church hymnbook, I wasn't sure if it was real or not. That's why, even to this day, I have to sit down and scour the Bible for myself and look up every little minute detail to prove things.*

*So when I saw what was happening in my husband's life, I exclaimed to his mother, Evelyn, "You're going to have to explain this one to me!"*

*But she just shook her head and told me, "Lindsay, I can't explain it." Then she added, "This isn't a new thing. This is an old thing." But the more she tried to explain it, the more jumbled up it seemed to get in my brain. It didn't make any sense to me!*

*I mean, Richard went to Lakeland, he brought home the video, and it was a whole new revelation to me. **But it was just a revelation of something that I was seeing. It hadn't hit me personally!** Then we went to the services at Rhema Bible Church, and Richard kept telling me, "Lindsay, stop trying to figure it all out! You'll never experience it until you stop* *trying to figure it out and let God be God."*

I said, *"Okay, fine."* But when I went to the services, honestly, I was still trying to figure it out! I was saying, *"Now how does he do that? What's he doing now? Is it happening because other people are laughing, and when they say something funny, does it trigger it?"* Oh, I had to have a logical explanation for everything!

But do you know what? As long as I kept on questioning it, it didn't do one single thing for me personally. Then SUDDENLY, God hit me with the joy of the Holy Spirit — not with laughter, tee-hee-hee, not with human emotions. But in my inner man, my spirit man, I felt a rush of the Holy Spirit, and the power of almighty God hit me with such a force that it was like someone had taken a baseball bat and hit me over the head with it!

Now I wasn't asking God for this experience. I wasn't even going to get involved if I couldn't figure it out first! Then if I did figure it all out, I was going to say, *"Okay, God, now You can hit me with it!"* But God chose to do it His way. **Thank God, He is God!**

All at once, when I wasn't paying the least bit of attention, SUDDENLY something exploded inside my being and the power of God came on me, and I fell to the ground laughing hysterically. At that precise moment all I wanted was what the Lord wanted for my life!

Now I'm the kind of person who would say, *"Oh, God would never do anything like that to me because He would never let me be so embarrassed in public."* **HA!** Never say never! You should have seen me! It was hilarious! What happened was that Lindsay let go and God took over. Suddenly, Lindsay was gone, and the experience of God was so almighty, so glorious, so big, that my problems were not my problems anymore. Oh, the problems still existed, but all the care had vanished! After two years of trying to do everything short of chopping off Richard's head to get him up out of the debt load, *in the flash of a second those burdens completely disappeared!*

Then suddenly — now hear me when I say that word SUDDENLY — God took over my life in a fresh new way. The glory of God, the presence of God, took over. I was on the floor laughing. I was rolling around in the aisles of the church. I was making a fool of myself — **a fool for Christ!**

I fell all over the church pew where Brother and Sister Hagin were sitting, and I was laughing and blubbering on the floor. Richard has known me for sixteen years now, and that is just not like me! I mean, it took me a long time, even being married to Richard Roberts, to raise my hands and clap in church. With my denominational background, I didn't believe in doing that. *And I still haven't danced in church!*

It's so hard for people to understand how someone who looks perfectly normal can suddenly appear to be so abnormal, rolling around on the floor, laughing hysterically. But, you see, God SUDDENLY poured out His Spirit on me. And when God pours out His Spirit on your life, something fantastic happens in the spirit realm.

Let me tell you a little story which may help you understand what I'm talking about. The other day our daughter Jordan was standing beside my bathtub, and she didn't realize that the shower button was up. When she turned on the bathwater, she suddenly got sprayed from head to toe. She got poured on. Well, *that's what happened with God and me. Suddenly, the Spirit of God poured Himself out onto my whole being. Suddenly, I got showered. I got hit with the power of the Spirit, and Lindsay disappeared and the Spirit of God took over.*

*And, friend, there's a suddenly for your life, too, if you'll only tell yourself, "Sit down, flesh; stand up, God." <u>THEN</u> GOD WILL POUR IT OUT ON YOU. But the real key is, <u>you've got to want what God has for you</u>.*

*I decided that I didn't want only what I could analyze. I didn't want only what I could reason out with my mind. I didn't want only what I had read about in a church hymnbook. SUDDENLY, I wanted whatever God had for my life. And when I opened myself up to the Lord, He literally hit me like a rocket booster, and the joy of the Lord came pouring into my life!*

*SUDDENLY, I didn't care how dignified I was or wasn't! What was happening to me was so much of God — and I KNEW it was of God — that I didn't care what people said or thought. I was in the awesome, holy presence of the Lord. I may have been laughing my head off, but as funny as it may have looked or seemed, I WAS TRULY 100 PERCENT IN THE PRESENCE OF THE LIVING GOD! <u>AND HE WAS DOING A MIGHTY WORK IN ME!</u>*

## GOD IS CUTTING THROUGH
## ALL THE RED TAPE OF MY LIFE!

This happy, hilarious, Holy Ghost laughter wasn't the only result of this outpouring of joy in my life. **The joy of the Lord brought a remarkable**

**change in me, a real reviving of my entire life.**
It was like the Bible says in Isaiah 43:18,19. God
caused a river of joy to spring up in the middle of a
scorching wasteland! He caused the parched, thirsty
desert of my life TO BLOSSOM LIKE A ROSE!

Not only has *my* life been transformed, but this
extraordinary explosion of holy joy and laughter has
been spreading like wildfire all around the world! It's
bringing a dramatic change in churches everywhere.
In Great Britain, this fresh move of the Holy Spirit
has come into four thousand churches. It's bringing
old-time revival and repentance into people's hearts!
It's bringing wholeness and holiness, and an incredible outpouring of signs and wonders, healing and
miracles!

One of the most gratifying by-products of the joy of
the Lord in my life was holy laughter from Heaven!
*And I've truly been laughing a lot!* I attended another
meeting at Rhema Bible Church here in the Tulsa
area, and Brother Kenneth Hagin, Sr., said to me,
"You know, I don't understand all this confusion
about people who laugh. When you're happy, you
laugh! ***What's so hard to understand about that?***"

Now I've seen some people in these amazing revival services who didn't utter even a single chuckle!
Some react the way Marilyn Hickey did at that first
meeting she attended in Denver. She was so over-
come by the awesome presence of the Lord that she
just wept and wept.

*And her experience is not an isolated one!* I've seen
countless numbers of people in these Holy Ghost
meetings with tears rolling down their cheeks — tears
of joy, tears of repentance, tears of cleansing! For me,
the most recent revival at ORU was an experience of

weeping uncontrollably in the presence of the Lord!

> **THE MESSAGE I'M DRIVING HOME TO YOU IS THIS: THE EMPHASIS IS NOT ON LAUGHTER. THE EMPHASIS IS ON <u>CHANGE</u> — A CHANGED HEART, A CHANGED LIFE.**

Didn't the psalmist David declare, "Purge me with hyssop. . . . Create in me a clean heart, O God" (Psalm 51:7,10)? David stumbled headlong into a pit of sin when he committed adultery with Bathsheba. But he cried out to the Lord, "Cleanse me from my iniquities!" (see Psalm 51:2). *I tell you, God is cleansing His people from their sins through this revolutionary outbreak of Holy Ghost joy!*

Sometimes I find myself being engulfed with happy, uncontainable, joy-filled laughter, and sometimes I find myself weeping in the awesome presence of the Lord. But <u>AFTER</u> the laughter and <u>AFTER</u> the weeping, I **<u>ALWAYS</u>** find myself changed in the depths of my soul. *REALLY, THE LORD IS CUTTING THROUGH ALL THE RED TAPE OF MY LIFE, LIFTING ME UP TO SERVE HIM WITH A MIGHTY SPIRIT OF JOY!*

Chapter 8

# THE PROOF OF THE PUDDING IS IN THE EATING!

Ever since the joy of the Lord swept over my life, God's healing power has come upon me so strongly that it almost takes my breath away! There has been a spontaneous leap in the number of miracles. *It's as if God is raising the level of anointing another notch higher so that more of His healing power can come streaming through!*

While I've been crisscrossing this nation from coast to coast with the Gospel, the gifts of the Spirit have been flowing in a greater measure than ever before. The word of knowledge and the gifts of healing and miracles are more evident now — not because of me BUT BECAUSE OF THIS FRESH OUTPOURING OF JOY FROM HEAVEN!

When the joy of the Lord washes over my soul, it's as if a supernatural valve is released in the spirit realm. God's mighty Holy Ghost power starts pumping through my life like a powerful, healing torrent. Miracles, signs and wonders, healings, and the gifts of the Spirit are breaking loose on every hand! Here is just a little taste of the outstanding victory reports I've been receiving:

# THE DOCTORS WERE PLANNING TO PULL THE PLUG, BUT GOD RAISED UP MY DAUGHTER!

*Richard, my daughter had emphysema, asthma, and pneumonia, and all the medication she was receiving had caused her body to swell up like a balloon from the fluid retention. The doctors were doing everything they could to help her, but nothing seemed to work. Things looked so bad that they were planning to pull the plug **and take her off the life-support system!***

*In the meantime, I was attending a conference you and Lindsay were hosting in Tulsa, and the joy of the Lord was breaking out everywhere. So I sent you a note, asking you to pray for my daughter, and I also requested prayer at the Prayer Tower. One of my daughters took a small cassette tape player into my dying daughter's hospital room and placed the earpiece in her ear. Then she began to play your tape, "He's a Healing Jesus."*

*I'm telling you, God reached down from Heaven that day and touched my daughter's body, and she came up out of that hospital bed, COMPLETELY HEALED! The doctors couldn't imagine what had happened! <u>But we knew what had happened!</u> **THE HOLY SPIRIT TOOK OVER, AND SHE WAS MIRACULOUSLY RAISED UP!***

Jewel from Ohio

# IT'S HARD TO BELIEVE IT'S THE SAME LEG!

*Richard, I attended one of Lindsay's Women's*

*Conferences where you called out a word of knowledge, saying, "Anyone who has bad knees, come down here right now." My left knee had been operated on three different times because of arthritis. The last time, the surgeon discovered that the back side of my kneecap had completely deteriorated and was rubbing against the thigh bone! So he finally had to remove the kneecap, and for twelve years I had not been able to bend that knee.*

*When you came down the prayer line to lay your hands on me, you asked, "Which knee is it?" After I told you about my surgeries, you prayed for me and down I went in the Spirit for almost one and a half hours! The power of God was all over me!*

*When I was able to get up, there were only a few people left in the building. One of your men helped me, and we started walking back and forth across the building to test my knees. Suddenly, I realized there was no more pain or stiffness! I COULD WALK NORMALLY! Then I started jumping up and down and praising God!* **IT'S HARD TO BELIEVE IT'S THE SAME LEG!**

Deloris from South Dakota

## PARTNER GETS A COMPLETE
## HOLY GHOST OVERHAUL
## FROM THE LORD!

*Richard, I was diagnosed with cancer of the cervix and also of the bladder, and the doctors told me that this kind of cancer can easily spread from one part of the body to another. I was able to attend your Partner brunch in San Antonio, Texas, and also the healing*

111

*service at Cornerstone Church. When you prayed for me, I was healed from the cancer in my bladder and cervix. But <u>that was only the beginning of my miracle</u>.*

*Next, my left ear opened, and I could hear clearly. Then a disk in the middle of my spine snapped into place. I was also healed from four aneurysms which were located in areas where the doctors couldn't operate on them. <u>But God still wasn't finished with my miracle</u>!*

*I received a healing of a flattening of the bone in my hip and right leg. <u>For the first time in nineteen years, I can walk without limping</u>! <u>MY RIGHT LEG IS NO LONGER TWO INCHES SHORTER THAN MY LEFT ONE</u>!* **I was so excited in the Spirit about my miracles that I just kept on praising Jesus and singing for an entire week!**

Siouxmara from Texas

## GOD SAID, "I'M GIVING YOU A LASER-LIKE ACCURACY IN THE OPERATION OF THE GIFTS OF THE SPIRIT!"

In August of 1994, I was slated to be a speaker for a ministers' conference in Florida, and I arrived at the meeting early because I was hungry to receive a fresh touch from the Lord. Now I had no earthly idea what God had in store for me, but whatever it was, *I WANTED TO REACH OUT AND GRAB AHOLD OF IT WITH EVERY FIBER OF MY BEING!*

Several thousand ministers had gathered for that particular session, and a local pastor was delivering a soul-stirring message straight from his heart. At the close of the service, a hush fell over the crowd when he gave an invitation for special prayer. Something leaped in my heart as I stepped toward the altar, ***because I wanted so desperately to receive from God!***

As that man passed by me, he suddenly began to prophesy, declaring by the Spirit, "I'm giving you a laser-like accuracy in the operation of the gifts of the Spirit that flow through your life, especially in the word of knowledge." Then he added, "It has always been strong in you, but now there will be a laser-like accuracy like you've never experienced before." Friend, it was a very potent word from the Lord, *and it seemed to burst into reality almost overnight!*

It was as if I had stepped into a brand-new dimension of the word of knowledge! All at once, I was able to zero in more accurately on the exact location of the person in the audience who was receiving God's touch. Sometimes the Lord would reveal the most minute details about who was being healed and exactly how they were feeling the anointing of His Spirit. I tell you, it has been almost more than I can fathom, ***AND I BELIEVE IT'S A DIRECT RESULT OF THE JOY OF THE LORD IN MY LIFE!***

Here are some more thrilling testimonies so you can see for yourself the amazing results of this word from the Lord:

## THE GROWTH ON THE BACK OF MY NECK POPPED OUT INTO THE PALM OF MY HAND!

*Richard, several months ago I woke up during the night and turned on the TV, and you and Lindsay were reading some testimonies on Trinity Broadcasting Network. When you finished, you told the viewers that if they had a need, they should touch something which represented that need while you prayed.*

*During your prayer, you said that a man was being healed from a growth or lump on his neck. Then you said that **IT WAS HEALED** and not to worry because the growth hadn't disappeared yet. You said that it wasn't the appointed time, but the growth was already healed. As you and Lindsay finished praying, I gave praise and glory to the Lord for my healing!*

*You see, I'd had a growth on my neck about the size of a Ping-Pong ball from the age of twelve or thirteen, and I am now forty-eight years old. I knew that the Lord healed me that night, so I didn't think anymore about it.*

*Several weeks later, I woke up again during the night, so I turned the TV on and started to watch Paul and Jan Crouch on TBN. Paul was talking about various preachers who were being persecuted by the "heresy hunters," and then he named a few who were being criticized, including your dad, Oral Roberts.*

*As soon as Paul said they were attacking the Roberts' ministry, that growth on the back of my neck popped right out into the palm of my hand! Richard, I believe the Lord healed me in this way to be a witness that God's hands ARE upon you and your ministry! You are truly a healing prophet of God!*

Joseph from Florida

## NOW I'M HEALED
## FROM THE TOP OF MY HEAD
## TO THE SOLES OF MY FEET!

*Richard, after experiencing homelessness and being abandoned by an abusive, alcoholic husband, I was finally able to get a job as a waitress. While working long hours — many ten- and twelve-hour shifts — I leaned over too far one day and something snapped in the arch of my right foot. I asked God to help me keep on working because I just couldn't face homelessness again. So I stepped out in faith and began speaking the Word of God and believing for my healing.*

*Each night I would go home and look at that lump in the arch of my foot as it swelled to the size of a quarter and completely filled my arch. This went on for two years, until one night I was watching you and Lindsay on TBN, and you said, "There's a lady out there watching. You've done something to the arch of your right foot. God is healing it now!" Glory to God, I watched that lump go down, and it has never swollen up again!* **Now I'm healed from the top of my head TO THE SOLES OF MY FEET!**

Mary from Georgia

## I CAUGHT A GLIMPSE OF A HAIR DRYER
## DRYING UP THE FLUID
## IN SOMEBODY'S LUNGS!

I get carried away in my spirit every time I think about the testimony a man shared with me at the Hagin Campmeeting here in Tulsa, Oklahoma, two years ago. Brother Kenneth Hagin, Sr., had called me up to the platform to preach, and after the service a man eagerly rushed to the front to give his testimony.

"Richard," he told me excitedly, "I've had fluid in my lungs for the last two months." And just at that moment, an image flashed through my mind of a very strong word of knowledge God had given me during that service. When I received that word, in my spirit I had caught a powerful glimpse of a hair dryer drying up the fluid in somebody's lungs!

When I described the picture God had dropped into my spirit, the man exclaimed, "That's exactly what happened! It has completely dried up! There's been so much fluid lately that I've been choking and coughing. I've even been struggling to talk. BUT NOW IT'S ALL DRIED UP! Glory be to God!"

## RICHARD, YOU DESCRIBED MY PROBLEM TO A T!

Friend, the praise report I'm about to share with you really lifts my spirits every time I share it! It's the testimony of the young woman I referred to earlier who came forward during the evening service in Lakeland, Florida. She had been tormented by an unbearable ringing in her ear for eight long years, and I want you to read her very heart-touching story in her own words:

*Richard, when you said there was someone here with an ear problem, I was flipping through my Bible, and suddenly, I stopped because I thought, "God is going to give me a healing!" I cannot describe to anyone the pain, except that there has been a popping* *and a static in my ear for almost eight years. When you gave that word, <u>you described it to a T</u>.*

While she was relating to me in graphic detail how God had miraculously healed her, like a bolt of lightning, the joy of the Lord hit me. Then it hit her, and I burst into such uncontrollable Holy Ghost laughter that I accidentally spit all over her! I mean, p-p-p-p-p-p, just showered her with spit! I was totally embarrassed and had to apologize! ***But I knew it was an outbreak of Holy Ghost joy, <u>and there was a double-portion outbreak of miracles as a direct result!</u>***

## THE JOY OF THE LORD HIT ME LIKE A RACING METEOR!

When the joy of the Lord hit my life in Lakeland, Florida, it struck with the force of a racing meteor! In only a matter of days, word began to spread all across America about the great things God was doing in my life! Since that time, I've been sharing about this anointed, power-packed Holy Ghost revival with our friends and Partners everywhere through a very special video entitled, *Joy, Joy, Joy!*

We've received countless testimonies from people whose lives have been transformed as they've witnessed this hilariously happy OUTPOURING of the Spirit — on our TV programs, in meetings, and through this special "Joy" video. And we've also heard from many who were healed as a result of this exciting new move of Holy Ghost joy! Here are just a few of those testimonies. ***I believe they're really going to bless your socks off!***

117

## I PRAY I WILL ALWAYS HAVE THIS WONDERFUL JOY!

*Richard, it has been a blessing watching you under the anointing of joy on your television program. I was standing in my kitchen recently when the Spirit of God came upon me, baptizing me with joy! My prayer language came flooding up out of me with the force of a tornado! I am praising God and praying that I will always have this wonderful joy!*

Earl from Ohio

## THERE ARE NO SIGNS OF SPLINTERED BONES ANYMORE!

*Richard, while I was watching your "Joy" video, I felt the anointing of God come all over me. All of a sudden, a healing came into my spine. You see, I've been suffering from splintered bones in my spine. But after watching your video, the doctor took new X rays,* **<u>and they show that my spine is completely healed!</u>** *THERE ARE NO SIGNS OF SPLINTERED BONES ANYMORE!*

Mrs. S. from New York

## IF YOU DON'T WANT THOSE HEADACHES, THEN GIVE THEM AWAY!

*Richard, for more than twenty years, I've been plagued by excruciating migraine headaches. They would start unexpectedly and become so debilitating* that I would suffer temporary blindness and nearly lose consciousness. Many times I've been hospitalized and heavily sedated with pain medication.

One day while I was watching A New Perspective, you had a word of knowledge about headaches being healed. I accepted that word for myself and began praising and thanking God for it. Then the Lord spoke in my heart and asked me, "How long do you want to keep those headaches?"

I said, "God, what do You mean, how long do I want to keep these horrible headaches? They're destroying my life!"

Then I heard the Lord speaking plainly in my spirit, "If you don't want them anymore, then give them away!"

Well, the joy of the Lord came upon me and I started to laugh! It was such a simple solution to such a seemingly unsolvable problem. So I spoke to the devil and said, "Satan, I'm giving you notice. I don't want those headaches from hell anymore! In the Name of Jesus, be gone and don't ever return!"

I felt a release in my spirit, and I knew they were gone! Now, many months later, <u>I still have no headaches</u>! My testimony has inspired so many people at my church THAT IT'S CAUSED JOY AND HOLY LAUGHTER TO SPREAD THROUGHOUT THE ENTIRE CONGREGATION!

Linda from Arkansas

## GOD'S JOY HAS GIVEN ME
## A BRAND-NEW PASSPORT TO LIFE!

I believe America and perhaps the entire world are ripe for a tremendous OUTPOURING of the joy of the

Lord! And one of the most outstanding by-products of this Holy Ghost joy in my life has been an astonishing *overflow* of healings and miracles!

I've felt the healing presence of the Lord moving through my life for many years, but God's Spirit is flowing through me now with an even greater force than ever before *since I've received this mighty, holy baptism of joy!*

Yes, there may be detractors, naysayers, and gainsayers, BUT THEY'VE COME TOO LATE FOR ME! You see, I've decided that I'm going to have a fullhearted measure of the joy of the Lord, even if a cyclone is sweeping through my life! I'm going to laugh hilariously, uncontrollably, with holy joy! *AND I'M GOING TO REJOICE WHILE THE LORD RAINS DOWN HIS MIRACLES FROM HEAVEN!*

It's too late for me to change! I've already crossed over the line! I'm going to stand up tall, square my shoulders, hold my head up, and let my heart be FILLED with spontaneous, uncontrollable joy! *WHEN I'M FULL OF JOY, THE WHOLE WORLD LOOKS DIFFERENT TO ME! GOD'S JOY HAS GIVEN ME A BRAND-NEW PASSPORT TO LIFE!*

# Chapter 9

# HOW I BECAME ANOTHER MAN

What a glorious moment it was when the prophet Samuel anointed Saul to be the first king of Israel — God's choice to be the ruler of His people. Now let me just set the scene for you as this dramatic story from the Bible unfolds.

First Samuel 10:1 declares, "Then Samuel took a vial of oil, and poured it upon his [Saul's] head, and kissed him." Now this is not referring to a sexual kiss. It's symbolic of the kiss of God coming upon Saul's life. And no doubt Samuel laid his hands upon the new king as he told him, *"The Spirit of the Lord will come upon you and you shall prophesy* . . . **and shall be turned into another man"** (I Samuel 10:6).

*Friend, if ever a Scripture was written for my life, it's this Scripture!* **I tell you, those words could have been written about my life today!** You see, I had no more earthly idea how to be the President of Oral Roberts University when was I first elected to that office than Saul had of how to be the king of Israel. But Samuel prophesied to him, "The Spirit of the Lord will come upon you."

When I stepped into the office of President of ORU, I felt totally inadequate to fill that position. Really, there was no way for me to grasp what it would be like to be the President and Chief Executive Officer of a world-class university. People could describe to me in graphic detail what it would be like, but until I moved into that position myself, there was no way I could imagine what it would entail. *It would be like trying to imagine what it's like to strap on a parachute and hurl yourself from an airplane. Until you actually strap on that parachute and take a flying leap into the sky, you have no idea what it's like!*

But my, have I received an education over these past few years! You see, I hold two degrees from Oral Roberts University — a bachelor's degree and a master's degree. But lately, I've received another degree — **the third degree. *That's the degree you receive from the school of hard knocks!***

So the Lord told Saul, "The Spirit of the Lord will come upon you," signifying that God would give him a fresh, new anointing to stand in the office of king. Ever since my father announced that he would step down as President of ORU, I have spent many intense hours in prayer, crying out to the Lord for *a double portion of His anointing. **And the Spirit of God has flooded my life with a powerful new anointing for that office!***

Then the Lord declared to Saul through the prophet Samuel, "And you will prophesy." Now the gift of prophecy is one of the nine gifts of the Holy Spirit described in I Corinthians 12, but I don't believe this is merely a word about the gift of prophecy. <u>*I believe it's a word about all nine gifts of the Spirit!*</u>

Samuel was saying, "Not only will the Spirit of the Lord come upon you, but the gifts of the Spirit will burst alive in your life!" And there's been a mighty EXPLOSION of the gifts of the Spirit surging through my life, especially during the past few years!

Not only has the operation of the word of knowledge increased dramatically but I've also begun to feel the power of the Lord burning and moving through my hands like never before! I feel a holy heat flowing through me, and yet there's no physical sign of redness. There's no fire, but suddenly there is a holy heat burning through my hands. *It's as if the Spirit of God is pumping through my hands like a powerful current of fire!*

The next word Samuel spoke to Saul just leaped out at me the very first moment I read it. I mean, my mouth fell open, and I exclaimed, **"This is my Scripture!"** The prophet told the brand-new king, *"You're going to be turned into another man!"*

Friend, over these last few years as President of Oral Roberts University, **I feel as if I've become another man**. In fact, my own wife has told me, "Richard, you're a different person now!" Even though my outward circumstances didn't turn around the instant I received the joy of the Lord, I CHANGED ON THE INSIDE. The Spirit of God came upon me, the gifts of the Spirit began flowing in a greater measure through my life, *AND I BECAME ANOTHER MAN!*

Now, of course, I was still dealing with some of the same nightmarish problems I was facing before. *But suddenly I was filled with a joy that lifted me above the turmoil.* I'm talking about a manifestation of holy joy and laughter that takes over your life, and you're not the same anymore! **Something new exploded in the life of Richard Roberts!** *I became a brand-new man because of the joy of the Lord!*

## YOU CAN BE CHANGED
## INTO ANOTHER MAN, ANOTHER WOMAN!

You may be thinking, *Richard, I want to become*

*another man, another woman, but I don't know where to begin!* <u>Oh, friend, the bottom line in life is in giving your life to Jesus</u>! Second Corinthians 5:17 declares that when you open your heart to the Savior, **you become a brand-new person.** *You're as different from the person you were before as the East is from the West!* ***A spiritual metamorphosis EXPLODES in your life!***

Or perhaps you've been warming the church pew on Sunday morning, but you don't have the peace of Christ for your lonely soul! My brother, my sister, young person, *you never know when your time will come!* If you lost your life tonight, would the devil snatch your soul away? I tell you, Jesus Christ died so that you could have a blood-bought, Heaven-sent, Holy Ghost salvation! Why don't you open your heart to Him right now as you pray this prayer out loud:

"O God, be merciful to me, a sinner, a backslider. I'm tired of all the games, the playacting, the empty charade. I believe there's a better world than this one just over the horizon, *AND I DON'T WANT TO MISS HEAVEN WHEN I DIE!* I repent of my sins, my wrongdoings. I renounce every tool that's holding me in satan's grip! I fling those things aside and open my heart to the Savior! ***By faith, I receive Him as the Lord of my life!***

"I'm turning loose of every stronghold of the devil's dark kingdom! In the mighty Name of Jesus, I'm rebuking satan at every door! I'm washed in the blood that's flowing down from Calvary's mountain! Jesus Christ is reigning on the throne of my life! *Through the shed blood of the Savior, I'm being changed into another person!* GOD'S JOY IS STREAMING DOWN ON ME LIKE A MIGHTY RAIN FROM

ABOVE! Amen."

The greatest day of my life was the day I gave my heart to Jesus! And if you just prayed that prayer with me, then you're about to step up to a thrilling new plateau in life! If you want to feel as if you're ten feet tall, *then Jesus Christ will make you feel as tall as Heaven!* Oh, can't you feel the moving of the Spirit? He's driving out the darkness *by turning on His light! And when the light of God comes blazing through,* **THE DARKNESS DOESN'T HAVE A CHANCE!**

If you've just received Jesus Christ as your Lord and Savior, I have a little book I want to send you, entitled, *How to Live Your New Life!* You can write to me, Richard Roberts, Tulsa, Oklahoma 74171, or if you live in Canada, Richard Roberts, Station K, Box 8, Toronto, Ontario M4P 2G2, or you can call the Abundant Life Prayer Group at (918) 495-7777.

## I WANT TO FINISH MY COURSE WITH JOY!

In Acts 20:24, the apostle Paul declared triumphantly, "But none of these things move me." What is he talking about here? None of these trials, these tribulations — none of these experiences of being whipped with rods, stoned with rocks, hurled into prison, and wrapped in cruel chains — *NONE OF THESE THINGS MOVE ME*.

Then he added, "Neither do I esteem my life dear to myself, IF ONLY I MAY FINISH MY COURSE WITH JOY, and the ministry which I have obtained of . . . the Lord Jesus, faithfully to attest the good news [Gospel] of God's grace" (AMPLIFIED).

**I tell you, that Scripture is the cry of my heart today, and I hope it's the cry of your heart too!** There's a sighing, crying, dying world out there, and they're going to be lost and damned forever unless you and I snatch them from the jaws of hell! *And if we're going to snatch them out of satan's grasp, WE'VE GOT TO HAVE THE JOY OF THE LORD WHICH IS OUR STRENGTH! Why?* **Because it's the joy of the Lord shining through our lives that draws the lost to Christ!**

Now you may be thinking, *Richard, I remember a time when my heart was full of joy, but I don't know how to sustain God's joy in my life!* Oh, I'm so glad you mentioned that subject because I've had every opportunity to let satan drive the joy right out of my life!

I mean, just because I had a visitation from God in the fall of 1993, turned a Holy Ghost somersault in midair, and experienced a mighty river of joy erupting down in my soul doesn't mean that I wake up every morning with a smile plastered across my face! No! I have countless opportunities to lose my joy *every day*, the same as you do!

There have been so many times over the last few years when the devil took deadly aim at Oral Roberts University, even as there was an ominous cloud of debt hanging over this place! In other words, I didn't just wake up one morning and all of a sudden — poof — everything was smooth sailing!

---

**What I'm saying to you is this: I have to stir up the joy of the Lord in my life exactly as you do!**

---

How do I stir up the joy of the Lord? How do I keep a joyous expectancy for miracles bubbling up in my soul? First of all, I stay in a powerful attitude of praise and worship. *Friend, I'm not going to wait for the rocks to cry out with their praise and worship to the Savior!* I'm going to shout my praise to God with a voice of thanksgiving! I'm going to let my worship ring out until the foundations of Heaven begin to shake! You see, praise and worship are a vital part of sustaining God's joy in my life, **_because the joy of the Lord doesn't just happen!_**

I have days like you do when my telephone rings early and the devil tries to blot out my joy with some kind of heartrending news. *But I've made a dogged, determined decision to finish my course with joy!*

The apostle Paul proclaimed in Philippians 3:14: "I press toward the mark for the prize of the high calling of God in Christ Jesus." And, like Paul, I've also made an uncompromising, Holy Ghost decision to press toward the mark for the prize!

When I climb into my car each morning, I begin my day by lifting my hands in the air to almighty God and thanking Him for His goodness, His mercy, and His awesome presence. Then I begin to worship the Lord unashamedly from the depths of my soul *because He is a God Who glories and revels in our praises!*

If I'm driving to the office, I usually pull off the road somewhere on the beautiful grounds of Oral Roberts University and begin to prayerfully meditate on the Word of God. As the leader of ORU and our ministry, I put on the whole armor of God *by faith* for our corporate body. (See Ephesians 6:10-18.)

First of all, I put on the powerful belt of truth so I can be a soul winner for the Lord Jesus Christ. Then

I put on my breastplate of righteousness to protect my heart, with which I believe upon the Savior. Next, I reach down and pull on my gospel shoes so I can trample boldly over the devil's roughest territory! And I also cover my head with the helmet of salvation, *bringing my mind into subjection to my spirit.*

Then I take my Bible in my hand, which is the sword of the Spirit, the Word of God. It's a powerful, razor-sharp weapon which I can use to cut the devil down to size! BY FAITH, I hold my shield of faith up high as if I'm fending off the fiery missiles of the evil one — shielding myself, my family, the university, and our ministry against all of his death-dealing blows!

Then I take what I believe is the seventh piece of my mighty, invincible, Holy Ghost armor, and I begin to pray in tongues and also interpret back to my mind by praying in English. Next I cover my wife and children, then our faculty, staff, students, and the entire ministry property with an invisible Holy Ghost prayer cover of protection! **Friend, I'm talking about a Bible-based method of sustaining the joy of the Lord in my life!**

Before I know it, no matter what kind of bad news the devil has hurled at me that day, no matter whether it appears that all of my hopes have been dashed to pieces, <u>my face is smiling</u>. The joy of the Lord is bubbling up in my heart and I'm looking the world straight in the eye!

I'm not simply going through some kind of empty, meaningless motions out there in the parking lot every morning. I'm engaged in high-powered spiritual warfare against the enemy of my soul! *You see, this divine, Holy Ghost joy and laughter packs a powerful wallop against the devil!*

And I'm also saying to the Lord, "Help me stir up the river of joy that's lying dormant in my heart!" It's like those old-style pumps we used to have many years ago. You had to pour a little cup of water in to prime the pump. You had to put a little water in so you could get a lot of water gushing back out! So when I'm out there in the parking lot every morning, I'm really priming my spiritual pump!

I'm doing what Paul described in Acts 26:2 when he declared, *"I think myself happy."* He made an earnest, wholehearted decision of his faith to think himself happy. In the same regard, there's a Holy Ghost decision maker on the inside of me, and I've made a decision of my faith that I'm not going to lose the joy of the Lord. ***AND I REFUSE TO LET THE DEVIL SNATCH IT AWAY FROM ME!***

There are some mornings when I may need to have a good old-fashioned "attitude adjustment." So I declare by faith, "Lord, I resist this rotten, stinking attitude. I recognize that this is a strategy of satan, and I refuse to give the devil any place in my life. I'm going to hold my head up, put my shoulders back, and have a heart full of joy and thanksgiving unto the Lord!"

The next thing I know, I'm breaking out into joy-filled, hilarious laughter right there in my car in the parking lot! If somebody were to drive by and glance over at me, they'd probably think, *Richard, you're crazy! You're out of your mind!* Yes, I <u>am</u> out of my mind, <u>but I'm not crazy</u>. ***I'm into my spirit, where God created me to be!***

Now don't misunderstand what I'm saying here. I'm not advocating acting weird or flaky. If I'm lifting my hands in worship and adoration to the Savior, singing praises to Jesus on the ORU parking lot, *most people have a vague idea of what I'm doing!* I'm not parading up and down the streets of downtown Tulsa, Oklahoma, making a spectacle of myself!

Of course, if the Spirit of God moves on me in downtown Tulsa, Oklahoma, then that's a different story. But I'm not talking about doing something that's strange or irrational. I'm talking about something that's based upon the rock-solid foundation of God's Word! ***I'm talking about something that's desperately needed if the church is going to SHINE in this sin-darkened world!***

## IT'S TIME TO PUT ON
## A BIGGER COAT!

Now you may be thinking, *Richard, I'm just not as strong a Christian as you are. I can't possibly discipline myself the way you can!* Friend, it's time for you to stand strong and come to grips with the cold realities of life. **It's time to square your shoulders and stand tall, lest you be trampled by the onslaught of satan that's being unleashed upon this earth!**

I remember a very soul-stirring sermon my dad used to preach, entitled, "Put on a Bigger Coat!" That means you're going to have to lengthen your tent cords like the Bible says to do in Isaiah 54:2. You're going to have to cast aside those paralyzing fears and enlarge the borders of your tent — *enlarge your vision of God's plan and purpose for your life!*

It's time to stop protesting, "I'm shy. I'm reticent. I'm too intimidated to do something like that!" You may be someone who cowers at the very sight of your own shadow, but God's Word proclaims: *"God has not given us a spirit of fear; but of power, and of love, and of a sound mind!"* (See II Timothy 1:7.) *OH, IT'S TIME FOR YOU TO BECOME ANOTHER MAN, ANOTHER WOMAN — TO BECOME THE PERSON GOD CREATED YOU TO BE!*

Or you may be someone who's sitting in the dark with your arms folded, staring at the ceiling and waiting for God to move. *My brother, my sister, this Christian life is no free ride!* There's no hocus-pocus to it. It's real. It takes grit, it takes faith, it takes fortitude, it takes God's grace, and it takes human determination. You've got to stiffen your will and have courage and backbone to stand up straight and tall for Jesus and do your part.

Now let me drive this thought home to you by relating a little story from Genesis, chapter 37. It's the story of Joseph, a young man who had enough grit, enough persistence, enough holy determination, to pursue the dream God had placed in his heart. All of his life, Joseph worked, toiled, and labored. He was always putting his hand to the plow.

He worked in his father's fields as a young man, tending the flocks. In Egypt, he labored long, burdensome hours as the overseer of Potiphar's household. And even when he was cast into a dark dungeon cell in Pharaoh's prison *through no fault of his own,* **HE WORKED.** The warden appointed him foreman of all of his fellow prisoners! *JOSEPH WAS A MAN WHO ALWAYS KNUCKLED DOWN AND DID HIS PART!* And you and I must be like Joseph and put mighty wings to our faith **because James 2:26 declares that faith without works is dead!**

Oh, I'm praying that you'll grab ahold of this with your whole heart <u>because I believe the time is short</u>. The Bible says that in the twinkling of an eye we'll be snatched from this earth, and we'll ride out of this world *to be with the Lord forever!* In the meantime, we've got to be bold-hearted, faith-filled believers in Jesus, raising up a mighty banner for the kingdom of God! ***<u>And we can't lift that blood-stained banner to the sky without a great big double dose of the joy of the Lord!</u>***

## I'M RIDING ON THE CREST OF GOD'S HOLY GHOST JOY!

I knew in an instant God was speaking to me when our dear friend Jan Crouch shared a special Scripture not long ago on Trinity Broadcasting Network's *Praise the Lord* program. It was one night when my dad and mother, Oral and Evelyn Roberts, were her guests and Jan was reading a passage from the book of Psalms. Now I want you to just buckle your seat belt as you read this Scripture for yourself because I believe it's going to hit home in your heart too!

> *In your day of trouble, may the Lord be with you! May the God of Jacob keep you from all harm. May he send you aid from his sanctuary in Zion. May he remember with pleasure the gifts you have given him, your sacrifices and burnt offerings. May he grant you your heart's desire and fulfill all your plans. May there be shouts of joy when we hear the news of your victory, flags flying with*

*praise to God for all that he has done for
you. MAY HE ANSWER ALL YOUR
PRAYERS!* (Psalm 20:1-5, The Living
Bible).

I tell you, when Jan Crouch spoke those words, it
was like an atomic bomb exploded in my spirit! It
struck such a strong chord in me that I thought to
myself, *That Scripture is for me!* And I've got news for
you from the throne room of God! **I believe that
Scripture is for you too!**

BY FAITH, the day is about to burst on the horizon
when ORU's wall of debt will tumble to the ground!
And when that day comes, THERE WILL BE SHOUTS
OF JOY! There will be flags streaming in the air!
There will be people rejoicing wildly, sending up a
roar of praise to almighty God for all the great things
He's done for us!

My mind flashes back to the time when ORU
received official accreditation and my dad proclaimed
a special celebration on the ORU campus. *Oh, what
a celebration it was!* Well, I believe we ought to have
an old-fashioned, hallelujah, Holy Ghost blowout on
the day ORU breaks free from debt! ***And I believe it's
not going to be too long, in the mighty Name of
the Savior!***

I have a dream flooding up in my heart today, a
dream for ORU. In my spirit, I see the debt being
totally ***wiped out!*** I see the infrastructure of the
university being completely rebuilt, *with every academic program on the cutting edge for God!* I see the
endowment beginning to mushroom, and I see brand-
new buildings exploding out of the ground!

Friend, I'm deadly serious about the future of Oral

Roberts University because there are countless lives hanging in the balance. I have a vision of these young people streaming from the doors of ORU to every nation, every tribe, every tongue, every people, spreading the good news of the Gospel throughout every man's world! *Oh, I see the brightest future that I've ever seen, and I give all the glory to God!*

Now you may be thinking, *Richard, where's your evidence for that?* **My faith is the evidence!** My faith is bursting out of my chest today because I've caught a glimpse of something incredible on the horizon — for Oral Roberts University *and for your life too!* But before God can hurtle those obstacles out of our path, we've got to have a great big double dose of the joy of the Lord!

Why? Because it was holy joy and laughter that opened a pipeline to God's power in my life! It was a happy, hilarious spirit of joy which produced a revolutionary change in me! In only two years' time, I've been transformed into another man, <u>AND THE DEBT AT ORU HAS BEEN SLASHED BY 50 PERCENT</u>! **I tell you, I've got living proof that the joy of the Lord works, <u>and I want to see it working in your life too</u>!**

Every time I'm hanging over the edge of a precipice, every time satan issues another death threat against ORU, I start laughing in the Spirit and praising Jesus, the Rock of my salvation, *and God continues to turn satan away from our door!* Now I'm free from that horrendous stress level. I'm free from those terrible ulcers that were plaguing me. *I'm riding on the crest of God's Holy Ghost joy!*

Meanwhile, ORU is being transformed! This ministry is being revolutionized. Our television program is being set on fire by the Spirit of God! Reports are streaming in from people all over the world who are rejoicing, saying, "The joy of the Lord has overtaken my life, AND I'M NOT THE SAME PERSON ANYMORE!"

## AREN'T YOU TIRED OF THE DEVIL HAVING A FIELD DAY ON TOP OF YOUR HEAD?

*Wouldn't you rather have a full dose of the joy of the Lord which is your strength? Oh, I can feel a mighty force of God's Spirit just bursting from my heart to pray for you right now:*

"Heavenly Father, in the Name of Your only Son, Jesus Christ of Nazareth, I pray for Your contagious, hilariously happy, Holy Ghost joy to come upon everyone who reads this book. Lord, I'm asking for a fresh baptism of the joy of the Lord to flood like a mighty torrent over their souls. Pour it out upon their heads, down their faces and their shoulders, and let it stream in rivers down to their feet. *LET THEM BE ENGULFED WITH A GREAT REVIVAL OF JOY!*

"Lord Jesus, Your Word declares that the joy of the Lord is our strength. In our own strength, we can't rise up and be a beacon that's set by the Lord upon a high hill. But with Your joy burning in our souls, we can wrench the very gates of hell OFF THEIR HINGES!

"Lord, some who are reading my words this very moment are floundering. They feel as if they've been swallowed up by struggles and heartaches. They're overshadowed by mountains so forbidding that there's no earthly way to vault over them. God, I know how that feels, but I also know the incredible, earthshaking, uncontainable joy that's BURSTING ALIVE in my heart!

"Friend, I pray for you today, for the amazing joy of Jesus to start splashing all over you! May it engulf you and come flooding up out of your soul to the Lord! Oh, just let that river of spontaneous laughter FLOW! Thank You, Lord Jesus! *It's coming! It's coming! God's Spirit is ushering in a new baptism of joy!*

"I pray for a divine, Holy Ghost infusion of heavenly joy and laughter to overtake you and overwhelm you from your head to your toes! When your life is invaded by the everlasting joy of Jesus, it's sovereign, it's supernatural, IT'S HILARIOUSLY, HAPPILY FUNNY! *And you'll be transformed into another person AS THE JOY OF THE LORD SWEEPS OVER YOUR LIFE! Amen.*"